BUILDING SERVERLESS APPLICATIONS WITH AWS LAMBDA

Design and Deploy Serverless Architectures Using AWS Lambda

THOMPSON CARTER

TABLE OF CONTENTS

Introduction

The rise of serverless computing has revolutionized how software is designed, built, and deployed. By abstracting away infrastructure management, serverless platforms like AWS Lambda empower developers to focus entirely on building functionality, enabling rapid innovation, scalability, and cost efficiency. This book, ***Building Serverless Applications with AWS Lambda: Design and Deploy Serverless Architectures Using AWS Lambda***, provides an in-depth exploration of the capabilities, challenges, and real-world applications of AWS Lambda, guiding readers from foundational concepts to advanced use cases.

Why Serverless?

Traditional computing paradigms often require developers to manage complex infrastructure, provision resources, and scale systems manually. This not only increases operational overhead but also diverts focus from delivering value to users. Serverless computing eliminates these barriers by offering a fully managed environment where resources are dynamically provisioned based on demand. AWS Lambda, as a flagship serverless service, exemplifies this transformation.

With serverless, developers benefit from:

- **Automatic Scalability**: Functions scale seamlessly with the number of requests, accommodating traffic spikes without manual intervention.
- **Cost Efficiency**: Pay-as-you-go pricing ensures costs are directly proportional to usage, with no idle charges.
- **Faster Development Cycles**: Focus solely on writing code while AWS handles infrastructure provisioning, maintenance, and scaling.

Serverless architecture is not just a technical shift; it is a philosophical change that emphasizes agility and minimalism in application design.

The Scope of This Book

AWS Lambda is more than just a tool—it's a gateway to building modern, event-driven architectures that interconnect a wide range of AWS services. This book demystifies AWS Lambda and serverless computing, offering readers a comprehensive roadmap to mastering this paradigm. Whether you're a developer new to AWS or a seasoned architect, this book provides valuable insights and practical knowledge.

Key highlights include:

- **Foundational Concepts**: Understand the principles of serverless computing, the architecture of AWS Lambda, and its role within the broader AWS ecosystem.

- **Hands-On Implementation**: Step-by-step guides and code examples demonstrate how to create, deploy, and manage serverless applications.
- **Advanced Use Cases**: Explore sophisticated applications, from real-time analytics to machine learning, IoT, and hybrid cloud deployments.
- **Best Practices**: Learn how to optimize performance, ensure security, and control costs in serverless environments.
- **Real-World Applications**: Case studies and success stories illustrate how serverless is transforming industries.

Who Should Read This Book?

This book is designed for:

- **Developers and Engineers**: Gain hands-on experience with AWS Lambda and serverless development.
- **Solution Architects**: Learn to design scalable, resilient serverless architectures.
- **Business Leaders**: Understand the strategic advantages of serverless technology for driving innovation.
- **Students and Enthusiasts**: Explore serverless computing as an essential skill for the future of technology.

No prior experience with AWS Lambda is required, though familiarity with basic cloud computing concepts will enhance your understanding.

How This Book is Structured

To ensure a comprehensive learning experience, the book is organized into logical sections, each building upon the previous one:

1. **Foundations**: Introduces serverless computing, the core concepts of AWS Lambda, and its integration with AWS services.

2. **Core Development**: Focuses on building, deploying, and managing Lambda functions, with practical examples for common use cases.

3. **Advanced Topics**: Explores cutting-edge serverless applications, including machine learning, real-time processing, and multi-cloud architectures.

4. **Best Practices and Optimization**: Provides actionable strategies for cost optimization, security, and monitoring in serverless environments.

5. **Future of Serverless**: Examines emerging trends, innovations, and how to prepare for the evolving landscape of serverless computing.

Why AWS Lambda?

AWS Lambda is the undisputed leader in the serverless space, offering unparalleled integration with AWS's suite of services. It supports a variety of programming languages, provides robust monitoring and debugging tools, and offers a global footprint for low-latency execution. This makes Lambda a versatile and powerful choice for businesses of all sizes, from startups to enterprises.

The Goal of This Book

The goal of this book is not just to teach you how to use AWS Lambda but to inspire you to think serverless. By the end of this book, you will have the knowledge and confidence to:

- Design scalable and efficient serverless applications.
- Integrate AWS Lambda with various AWS and third-party services.
- Solve complex business challenges with innovative serverless solutions.
- Stay ahead in the ever-evolving cloud computing landscape.

Serverless is more than a toolset; it's a new way of thinking about technology. This book invites you to embark on a journey that will not only elevate your technical skills but also empower you to harness the full potential of serverless computing for your career, your organization, and the future of technology.

Welcome to the future of application development. Let's build something extraordinary!

Chapter 1: Introduction to Serverless Architecture

Overview of Serverless Computing

Serverless computing represents a paradigm shift in the way applications are developed and deployed. Unlike traditional architectures, where developers must provision, scale, and maintain servers, serverless computing abstracts away the underlying infrastructure. This abstraction allows developers to focus purely on writing and deploying code.

1. **Defining Serverless Computing**:
   - Serverless does not mean "no servers"; rather, it implies that developers don't need to manage servers directly.
   - Instead of managing hardware, software, and operational tasks, serverless computing relies on cloud providers to handle these aspects.

2. **How Serverless Works**:
   - Applications are broken into smaller units, typically functions, which are executed in response to specific triggers or events.

- o Popular services like AWS Lambda, Google Cloud Functions, and Azure Functions exemplify this model.

3. **Serverless vs Traditional Models**:
   - o **Traditional Model**: Requires setting up servers, configuring operating systems, and maintaining uptime.
   - o **Serverless Model**: Developers write code, and the cloud provider ensures the code runs when triggered, scaling resources as needed.

4. **Key Characteristics**:
   - o Event-driven architecture: Functions execute only in response to events.
   - o Scalability: Automatically adjusts based on workload without manual intervention.
   - o Pay-as-you-go pricing: Users pay only for actual execution time, not idle server time.

Benefits of Serverless Architecture

Serverless architecture offers a host of benefits that are revolutionizing the development and deployment of applications.

1. **Reduced Operational Overhead**:

- o No need to manage server maintenance, patching, or scaling.
- o Cloud providers handle updates, load balancing, and infrastructure health.

2. **Cost Efficiency**:
   - o Traditional servers run 24/7, incurring costs even during idle periods.
   - o Serverless charges are based solely on execution time and resources used, eliminating wasted expenses.

3. **Scalability**:
   - o Automatic scaling ensures that applications can handle sudden spikes in demand.
   - o Example: An e-commerce website during a flash sale can seamlessly scale up to handle millions of requests and scale down after the event.

4. **Faster Time to Market**:
   - o Developers can focus on core functionality rather than infrastructure.
   - o Rapid prototyping becomes easier, encouraging innovation.

5. **Environmentally Friendly**:
   - o By using resources only when needed, serverless architectures minimize energy consumption compared to always-on servers.

6. **Global Reach**:
   - o Deploying serverless functions across multiple regions is straightforward, enabling applications to serve users globally with low latency.

Challenges of Serverless Architecture

While serverless offers compelling benefits, it is not without challenges. Understanding these limitations is crucial for making informed architectural decisions.

1. **Cold Start Latency**:
   - o Serverless functions may experience delays during the first execution, as the infrastructure initializes the function.
   - o Example: A Lambda function invoked after a period of inactivity might take longer to execute.
2. **Vendor Lock-In**:
   - o Applications tightly coupled with a specific provider's serverless framework may face difficulties migrating to other platforms.
3. **Debugging and Monitoring**:
   - o Distributed nature of serverless applications complicates debugging and tracing.

- o Tools like AWS X-Ray can help, but they require additional setup.

4. **Execution Limits**:

- o AWS Lambda, for instance, imposes a maximum execution time of 15 minutes, which may not suit all workloads.

- o Resource constraints may also limit processing-heavy tasks.

5. **Security Concerns**:

- o Shared infrastructure can raise concerns about data security and compliance.

- o Proper IAM (Identity and Access Management) configurations are essential.

Key Use Cases for Serverless Solutions

Serverless architectures are ideal for a range of applications, from simple APIs to complex workflows.

1. **Web Applications**:

- o Example: A serverless backend for a social media platform that processes user posts, images, and notifications.

- o Benefits: Scalability and low operational costs make serverless ideal for fluctuating traffic patterns.

2. **Data Processing Pipelines**:
   - Use case: Processing and analyzing large datasets in real time.
   - Example: A system using AWS Lambda to process streaming data from IoT devices and store insights in a database.

3. **RESTful APIs**:
   - Serverless APIs handle CRUD (Create, Read, Update, Delete) operations efficiently.
   - Example: A mobile app backend that connects to a DynamoDB database via AWS API Gateway and Lambda.

4. **Real-Time Applications**:
   - Example: Real-time chat applications powered by WebSocket APIs with serverless backend logic.
   - Benefits: Dynamic scaling ensures a seamless experience during peak usage.

5. **IoT Applications**:
   - Example: A serverless pipeline for managing IoT sensor data, processing events in real-time, and storing results for visualization.
   - Benefits: Minimizes latency while ensuring scalability.

6. **Event-Driven Workflows**:

- o Example: An e-commerce site that triggers inventory updates when a purchase is made.
- o Benefits: Event-driven design ensures real-time updates without delays.

7. **Automation and Task Scheduling**:
   - o Example: Automated nightly backups of a database or processing logs.
   - o Serverless solutions like AWS EventBridge or CloudWatch rules can trigger Lambda functions on a schedule.

8. **Chatbots and Virtual Assistants**:
   - o Example: Using Lambda with AWS Lex to power conversational interfaces.
   - o Benefits: Simplifies the integration of AI-powered interactions.

9. **Serverless Machine Learning**:
   - o Example: Deploying ML models to predict product recommendations or analyze sentiment.
   - o AWS Lambda can invoke SageMaker endpoints for real-time predictions.

10. **Gaming Backends**:
   - o Example: A serverless architecture for handling multiplayer matchmaking and game state synchronization.

o Benefits: Serverless scales dynamically, ensuring consistent performance for players worldwide.

This comprehensive overview introduces the reader to the fundamentals of serverless computing, emphasizing its transformative potential and practical applications. Each section is backed by real-world examples to ensure clarity and relevance.

Chapter 2: Getting Started with AWS Lambda

What is AWS Lambda?

AWS Lambda is a serverless computing service provided by Amazon Web Services (AWS). It allows developers to execute code in response to events without the need to provision or manage servers. AWS Lambda automatically handles scaling, maintenance, and execution, letting developers focus solely on their application's logic.

1. **Core Concept**:
   - Lambda functions are small, single-purpose code snippets triggered by events.
   - For example, a Lambda function could execute automatically when a user uploads a file to an Amazon S3 bucket.

2. **How AWS Lambda Works**:
   - **Trigger**: An event occurs, such as an HTTP request through API Gateway or a database update in DynamoDB.
   - **Execution**: AWS Lambda runs the corresponding code in a secure, isolated environment.

- o **Automatic Scaling**: Lambda scales seamlessly to handle a single request or millions of concurrent requests.

3. **Key Features**:
   - o **Pay-As-You-Go Pricing**: Costs are based on execution time and memory usage.
   - o **Support for Multiple Languages**: Supports Python, Node.js, Java, Go, and others.
   - o **Event-Driven Model**: Triggers from over 200 AWS and third-party services.

4. **Real-World Use Cases**:
   - o Automating image resizing: Lambda can resize and save images when uploaded to an S3 bucket.
   - o Building RESTful APIs: Use API Gateway and Lambda to create scalable, serverless APIs.
   - o Processing data streams: Analyze real-time data from IoT devices or clickstream logs.

Setting Up Your AWS Account

To use AWS Lambda, you need an active AWS account. Setting up your account is straightforward and involves a few essential steps.

1. **Sign Up for AWS**:

- o Visit AWS's official website and click on "Create an AWS Account."
- o Provide your email address, a strong password, and a unique account name.
- o Complete the sign-up form with billing information and verify your identity.

2. **Choose a Support Plan**:
   - o AWS offers several support plans, from the free **Basic Support** plan to the more advanced **Enterprise Support**. Start with the free plan if you're new to AWS.

3. **Activate Your Account**:
   - o After completing the setup, AWS will verify your account via email or text.
   - o Once verified, your account will be active, and you can access the AWS Management Console.

4. **Set Up IAM for Security**:
   - o **Why IAM?** AWS Identity and Access Management (IAM) helps secure your account by controlling access to services and resources.
   - o Create an IAM user with limited permissions for daily use instead of using the root account.
   - o Assign policies such as AWSLambdaFullAccess to allow specific actions on AWS Lambda.

Exploring the AWS Management Console

The AWS Management Console is the web-based interface where you interact with AWS services, including AWS Lambda. Let's explore its layout and key features.

1. **Dashboard Overview**:
   - After logging in, the console's homepage provides a high-level view of your resources and commonly used services.
   - Use the **search bar** at the top to find AWS Lambda quickly.

2. **Navigating to AWS Lambda**:
   - In the Services menu, locate "Compute" and select **AWS Lambda**.
   - The Lambda service page displays options to create, manage, and monitor functions.

3. **Creating Your First Lambda Function**:
   - **Step 1: Define a Function**:
     - Click on "Create Function" and choose between these options:
       - **Author from scratch**: Write a new function using a runtime like Python or Node.js.

- **Use a blueprint**: Start with preconfigured templates for common use cases.
- Give your function a meaningful name (e.g., ImageProcessorFunction).

- **Step 2: Configure Runtime and Permissions**:
  - Choose a runtime such as Python 3.9 or Node.js 16.x.
  - Assign an IAM role or create a new one to define the permissions required by your function.

- **Step 3: Write or Upload Code**:
  - Use the in-console editor to write a basic "Hello, World" function, or upload a .zip package or container image with your code.

- **Step 4: Test Your Function**:
  - Create a test event (e.g., an S3 upload or a scheduled event) and execute the function to verify it works.

4. **Understanding the AWS Lambda Console Features**:
   - **Functions Tab**: View and manage all your Lambda functions.
   - **Layers**: Create shared libraries to optimize code reuse across multiple functions.

- o **Monitoring**: Use CloudWatch to visualize logs and metrics such as execution time, errors, and invocations.

5. **Hands-On Walkthrough**:

- o For beginners, create a simple function that responds with "Hello, World" when invoked:

python

```
import json

def lambda_handler(event, context):
    return {
        'statusCode': 200,
        'body': json.dumps('Hello, World!')
    }
```

- o Test the function using the AWS Lambda console by creating a dummy event, such as a JSON object.

Chapter 2 introduces the foundational steps to get started with AWS Lambda, from understanding its purpose to setting up your environment and creating a simple function. By the end of this chapter, readers will have a functional AWS account, familiarity with the AWS Management Console, and the confidence to experiment with their first Lambda function.

Chapter 3: AWS Lambda Core Concepts

Understanding Functions as a Service (FaaS)

Functions as a Service (FaaS) is the foundational concept of AWS Lambda. It represents a model where developers write and deploy single-purpose, event-driven functions without worrying about the underlying infrastructure.

1. **What is FaaS?**
    - o FaaS allows developers to execute code in response to specific triggers (e.g., an HTTP request or a file upload).
    - o Unlike traditional applications, FaaS focuses on writing smaller, modular code units that handle specific tasks.
2. **How FaaS Differs from Traditional Models**:
    - o **Traditional Applications**:
        - ▪ Typically monolithic and hosted on dedicated servers.
        - ▪ Require manual scaling, resource allocation, and server maintenance.
    - o **FaaS**:
        - ▪ Breaks functionality into smaller, deployable units.

- Automatically scales based on workload.

3. **Advantages of FaaS**:

   o **Efficiency**: No need to manage or maintain servers.

   o **Cost Savings**: Pay only for execution time; no charges for idle resources.

   o **Scalability**: Functions can scale independently without affecting other parts of the system.

4. **Examples of FaaS in Action**:

   o **Real-Time File Processing**: A function processes image uploads to an S3 bucket by resizing them or adding watermarks.

   o **Notification Services**: A function sends SMS or email notifications triggered by database updates.

   o **Data Aggregation**: A function aggregates IoT sensor data and stores it in DynamoDB for analysis.

Key Components of AWS Lambda

Understanding the components of AWS Lambda is crucial for leveraging its full potential.

1. **Functions**:

   o A Lambda function is the core executable unit in AWS Lambda.

- o Written in supported languages such as Python, Node.js, Java, Go, and more.

2. **Event Source**:
   - o Events trigger Lambda functions.
   - o Examples include:
     - An HTTP request via API Gateway.
     - A file upload to an S3 bucket.
     - A database update in DynamoDB.

3. **Execution Environment**:
   - o AWS Lambda runs your function in a secure, isolated runtime environment.
   - o Includes:
     - The operating system and runtime for your chosen programming language.
     - Temporary storage for operations requiring file handling.

4. **Permissions (IAM Roles)**:
   - o IAM roles define what actions a Lambda function can perform and on which AWS resources.
   - o Example:
     - A function processing S3 files needs an IAM role with permissions to read from and write to S3.

5. **Layers**:

- Layers are reusable components, such as libraries, that can be shared across multiple Lambda functions.
- Example:
  - A common utility library for logging or data validation.

6. **Concurrency and Scaling**:
   - AWS Lambda automatically scales based on the number of incoming requests.
   - **Concurrency**: Controls how many instances of a function can run simultaneously.

7. **Pricing**:
   - Based on:
     - Number of requests: $0.20 per 1 million requests.
     - Execution time: Calculated in milliseconds based on the memory allocated.

8. **Monitoring and Logging**:
   - **CloudWatch** provides logs and metrics for monitoring function execution.
   - Metrics include:
     - Number of invocations.
     - Duration of execution.
     - Errors and throttling.

Event-Driven Programming Basics

Event-driven programming is at the heart of AWS Lambda. In this model, actions (events) trigger corresponding responses (functions).

1. **What is Event-Driven Programming?**
   - A programming paradigm where code execution is triggered by specific events.
   - Events can originate from various sources, such as user actions, system changes, or external systems.

2. **Types of Events in AWS Lambda**:
   - **Asynchronous Events**: Events are queued for processing and executed independently of the source.
     - Example: An image uploaded to S3 triggers a Lambda function to process it.
   - **Synchronous Events**: The event source waits for a response from the Lambda function.
     - Example: API Gateway triggering a Lambda function for an HTTP request.
   - **Stream-Based Events**: Data streams, such as those from Kinesis or DynamoDB, trigger functions in real time.
     - Example: A Kinesis data stream triggers a function to process log entries.

3. **Common Event Sources**:
   - **AWS S3**:

- Event: File upload or delete.
- Example Use Case: Automatically resize uploaded images.

o **API Gateway**:
- Event: HTTP request.
- Example Use Case: Build RESTful APIs for a web application.

o **DynamoDB Streams**:
- Event: Insert, update, or delete operations.
- Example Use Case: Synchronize data changes to an external database.

o **EventBridge (CloudWatch Events)**:
- Event: Scheduled tasks or custom events.
- Example Use Case: Trigger daily backups or alerts.

o **SNS/SQS**:
- Event: Messages in a queue or topic.
- Example Use Case: Send notifications to users or process queued tasks.

4. **Designing an Event-Driven System**:

o **Decoupling**:
- Break down the application into smaller, independent components that communicate via events.

- Example: A purchase system where order processing, payment, and notifications are separate functions triggered by specific events.

    o **Real-Time Processing**:

    - Build systems that process events as they occur.

    - Example: IoT sensors streaming data to Lambda functions for immediate analysis.

5. **Practical Example: Event-Driven Workflow**:

    o Use Case: A simple photo-sharing app.

        1. User uploads a photo to an S3 bucket.

        2. An event triggers a Lambda function to process the image (e.g., resize or apply filters).

        3. The function stores the processed image in another S3 bucket.

        4. Another event triggers a notification service to alert the user that the image is ready.

This chapter introduces the foundational concepts of AWS Lambda, including the principles of Functions as a Service, key components, and event-driven programming. With these insights, readers can understand how AWS Lambda operates and how to design serverless applications driven by real-world events.

Chapter 4: Writing Your First Lambda Function

This chapter provides a hands-on introduction to creating, deploying, and testing your first AWS Lambda function. The goal is to get readers comfortable with the AWS Lambda workflow and understand its runtime environments.

Creating a Simple Lambda Function Using the AWS Console

AWS Lambda simplifies the process of creating and deploying serverless functions. In this section, we'll create a "Hello, World" Lambda function.

1. **Accessing the Lambda Console**:
   - Log in to the AWS Management Console.
   - Navigate to the **AWS Lambda** service under the "Compute" section.
2. **Steps to Create a Lambda Function**:
   - Click **Create Function**.
   - Select **Author from Scratch**.
   - Fill in the following fields:
     - **Function Name**: HelloWorldFunction.
     - **Runtime**: Select a supported runtime (e.g., Python 3.9 or Node.js 16.x).

o **Permissions**:

- Select **Create a new role with basic Lambda permissions**.

- This will automatically create an IAM role allowing the function to write logs to CloudWatch.

3. **Writing the Function**:

   o In the Lambda editor, you'll see a pre-filled function template. Replace it with the following code:

   - **Python**:

   python

   ```python
   import json

   def lambda_handler(event, context):
       return {
           'statusCode': 200,
           'body': json.dumps('Hello, World!')
       }
   ```

   - **Node.js**:

   javascript

   ```javascript
   exports.handler = async (event) => {
       return {
           statusCode: 200,
           body: JSON.stringify('Hello, World!')
   ```

```
    };
};
```

4. **Save and Deploy**:
   - Click **Deploy** to save your changes.
   - Your function is now ready to be tested.

Understanding the Runtime Environments

AWS Lambda supports multiple runtimes, providing flexibility in programming language and execution environment.

1. **What Is a Runtime?**
   - A runtime is the execution environment for your Lambda function, consisting of an operating system, programming language, and libraries.

2. **Supported Runtimes**:
   - AWS Lambda supports popular languages, including Python, Node.js, Java, Go, Ruby, and .NET Core.
   - Each runtime comes preconfigured with the necessary dependencies to execute functions in that language.

3. **Choosing the Right Runtime**:
   - Consider language familiarity, performance needs, and available libraries.
   - Example:

- Use Python for data processing tasks due to its rich ecosystem of libraries.
- Use Node.js for web APIs due to its asynchronous nature.

4. **Environment Variables**:
   o Runtimes allow you to set environment variables to pass configuration data to your function.
   o Example:
      - Storing API keys or database connection strings as environment variables.

5. **Execution Context**:
   o Each function execution includes the following:
      - **Temporary Storage**: Functions have access to /tmp storage (up to 512 MB) for temporary file operations.
      - **AWS SDK**: Preinstalled in some runtimes, simplifying integration with AWS services.

6. **Custom Runtimes**:
   o If your preferred language or runtime isn't supported, you can create a custom runtime using AWS Lambda layers.

Deploying and Testing Your First Function

After creating the function, it's essential to test it to ensure it works as expected.

1. **Creating a Test Event**:
   - Go to your function's page in the AWS Console.
   - Click **Test** and create a new test event.
   - Select **Hello World** from the template options or define your own JSON payload:

   json

   ```json
   {
       "key1": "value1",
       "key2": "value2",
       "key3": "value3"
   }
   ```

   - Save the test event with a name like TestEvent1.

2. **Executing the Function**:
   - After creating the test event, click **Test** to invoke the function.
   - View the results in the **Execution Results** section:
     - **Status Code**: 200
     - **Response Payload**: "Hello, World!"
   - Logs from the execution will be available in the **Logs** tab or via AWS CloudWatch.

3. **Exploring CloudWatch Logs**:

- o Navigate to the **Monitoring** tab and view the **Logs** link.
- o Examine logs to understand execution details, including:
  - Start and end times.
  - Memory usage.
  - Errors or warnings.

4. **Deploying to Production**:
  - o When deploying a function for production, consider the following:
    - **Environment Variables**: Use them to customize the function for different environments (e.g., dev, staging, prod).
    - **Concurrency Settings**: Configure concurrency limits to control costs and resource usage.
    - **Versioning and Aliases**: Use versioning to track changes and aliases to manage production and testing stages.

Real-World Example: Creating a File Processor

As a practical application, let's create a Lambda function that processes files uploaded to an S3 bucket.

1. **Use Case**:

   o A user uploads a file to an S3 bucket, and the Lambda function reads the file, processes its content (e.g., logs the data), and saves the output to another bucket.

2. **Steps**:

   o Create an S3 bucket named input-files.

   o Create another bucket named processed-files.

   o Write a Lambda function with the following code (Python example):

   python

```python
import boto3

s3 = boto3.client('s3')

def lambda_handler(event, context):
    for record in event['Records']:
        bucket = record['s3']['bucket']['name']
        key = record['s3']['object']['key']

        # Download the file
        download_path = f'/tmp/{key}'
        s3.download_file(bucket, key, download_path)

        # Process the file (example: log its content)
        with open(download_path, 'r') as file:
            data = file.read()
            print(f"File content: {data}")
```

```
# Upload the file to another bucket
output_bucket = 'processed-files'
s3.upload_file(download_path, output_bucket, key)


return {'status': 'Success'}
```

- o Configure an S3 event trigger for the input-files bucket to invoke the Lambda function on file uploads.

3. **Test**:
   - o Upload a file to the input-files bucket and verify that the function processes it and uploads the result to the processed-files bucket.

This chapter introduces readers to the practical steps of creating, deploying, and testing Lambda functions using the AWS Console. By the end of this chapter, readers will have the skills to write simple functions, understand runtime environments, and deploy working solutions. Each concept builds a foundation for developing more complex serverless applications in subsequent chapters.

Chapter 5: Events and Triggers in AWS Lambda

AWS Lambda thrives on its ability to respond to various event sources, making it a cornerstone of event-driven architectures. This chapter explores the wide range of event sources that AWS Lambda supports, walks you through setting up triggers, and provides real-world examples to inspire your applications.

Exploring Supported Event Sources

AWS Lambda integrates seamlessly with numerous AWS services and third-party tools, making it highly versatile for different use cases.

1. **Categories of Event Sources**:
   - **AWS Services**: Events triggered by services like S3, DynamoDB, and API Gateway.
   - **Scheduled Events**: Cron-like jobs created with EventBridge or CloudWatch Events.
   - **Custom Events**: Events generated by your application or external systems.
2. **Popular Event Sources**:
   - **Amazon S3**:
     - Events: ObjectCreated, ObjectRemoved.

- Example: Trigger a Lambda function to process images or videos uploaded to an S3 bucket.

  o **Amazon DynamoDB Streams**:
    - Events: Insert, update, or delete operations in a DynamoDB table.
    - Example: Synchronize data changes to an external database.

  o **Amazon API Gateway**:
    - Events: HTTP requests routed through API Gateway to Lambda.
    - Example: Build RESTful APIs using Lambda as the backend.

  o **Amazon SQS**:
    - Events: Messages added to an SQS queue.
    - Example: Process order requests queued in SQS.

  o **Amazon EventBridge**:
    - Events: Scheduled or custom events.
    - Example: Trigger a daily backup process at midnight.

  o **Amazon SNS**:
    - Events: Messages published to an SNS topic.
    - Example: Send notifications to subscribers when new content is uploaded.

3. **Third-Party Event Sources**:
   - ○ AWS Lambda can process events from third-party services using AWS Partner integrations or via HTTP endpoints.

4. **Custom Applications**:
   - ○ Applications can trigger Lambda functions programmatically using the AWS SDK.

Setting Up AWS Services as Triggers

Configuring AWS services as event sources for Lambda is straightforward. Let's explore how to set up triggers for three common services: S3, DynamoDB, and API Gateway.

1. **Amazon S3 as a Trigger**:
   - ○ **Use Case**: Automatically process uploaded files.
   - ○ **Steps**:
     1. Create an S3 bucket (e.g., upload-bucket).
     2. Navigate to your Lambda function in the AWS Management Console.
     3. Under the **Configuration** tab, select **Triggers** and click **Add Trigger**.
     4. Select **S3** as the trigger type.
     5. Choose your bucket and specify the event type (e.g., ObjectCreated).

6. Save the trigger.

o **Example**: A Lambda function that resizes images and stores them in another bucket.

2. **Amazon DynamoDB Streams as a Trigger**:

   o **Use Case**: React to database changes in real-time.

   o **Steps**:

      1. Enable DynamoDB Streams for your table.

      2. Choose the type of stream to capture (KeysOnly, NewImage, OldImage, or New and Old Images).

      3. In your Lambda function, add DynamoDB Streams as a trigger and configure the stream ARN.

   o **Example**: A function that logs all updates to a DynamoDB table.

3. **Amazon API Gateway as a Trigger**:

   o **Use Case**: Build a serverless REST API.

   o **Steps**:

      1. Create a new API in API Gateway.

      2. Define an HTTP method (e.g., GET or POST) and link it to your Lambda function.

      3. Deploy the API to a stage (e.g., prod).

   o **Example**: A Lambda function that returns JSON responses for a client-side application.

4. **Scheduling with Amazon EventBridge**:

- o **Use Case**: Trigger Lambda functions at regular intervals.
- o **Steps**:
    1. Navigate to EventBridge and create a rule.
    2. Define a schedule expression (e.g., cron(0 0 * * ? *) for midnight daily).
    3. Add your Lambda function as the target.

Real-World Examples of Event-Driven Applications

Event-driven architectures are powerful for building responsive, scalable, and efficient applications. Below are some real-world examples showcasing the versatility of AWS Lambda.

1. **Image Processing Pipeline**:
    - o **Scenario**: A photography platform that processes user-uploaded images.
    - o **Workflow**:
        1. User uploads an image to an S3 bucket.
        2. S3 triggers a Lambda function to resize and optimize the image.
        3. The processed image is stored in another S3 bucket.
    - o **Benefits**: Scales seamlessly for high upload volumes.
2. **Real-Time Data Processing**:

- o **Scenario**: A fitness app that tracks data from IoT devices.
- o **Workflow**:
  1. IoT devices send data to an Amazon Kinesis stream.
  2. Kinesis triggers a Lambda function to process the data.
  3. The processed data is stored in DynamoDB for visualization.
- o **Benefits**: Handles high-frequency data streams efficiently.

3. **Serverless REST API**:
   - o **Scenario**: A food delivery app that requires an API for managing orders.
   - o **Workflow**:
     1. API Gateway routes HTTP requests to Lambda functions.
     2. Lambda functions interact with DynamoDB to fetch or update order data.
   - o **Benefits**: Eliminates the need for traditional server maintenance.

4. **Notification System**:
   - o **Scenario**: An e-commerce site sends notifications for order updates.
   - o **Workflow**:

1. DynamoDB Streams detect changes in the Orders table.
2. A Lambda function sends notifications via SNS to customers.

- **Benefits**: Real-time notifications improve customer satisfaction.

5. **Automated Security Alerts**:

- **Scenario**: A company monitors suspicious activity in its cloud environment.
- **Workflow**:
  1. AWS CloudTrail logs events like unauthorized access attempts.
  2. CloudTrail triggers an EventBridge rule.
  3. The rule invokes a Lambda function to send alerts to the security team.
- **Benefits**: Quick response to security threats.

Events and triggers are the lifeblood of AWS Lambda, enabling it to respond dynamically to a vast array of scenarios. This chapter has covered the range of supported event sources, the steps to set up common triggers, and real-world applications that illustrate the power of event-driven architectures. With this understanding, you're equipped to design and implement serverless solutions that are both efficient and scalable.

Chapter 6: Integrating AWS Services with Lambda

AWS Lambda is designed to integrate seamlessly with a wide array of AWS services, enabling the creation of robust, scalable, and event-driven workflows. This chapter dives into how Lambda interacts with services like Amazon S3, DynamoDB, and SNS, explores how to build event-driven workflows, and showcases real-world use cases for these integrations.

Using S3, DynamoDB, and SNS with Lambda

AWS Lambda provides native support for integrating with many AWS services. Let's examine how to leverage these integrations effectively.

---

1.   Amazon   S3   and   Lambda

Amazon S3, AWS's object storage service, is often used with Lambda for file and data processing.

- **How It Works**:
  - Events such as file uploads (s3:ObjectCreated) or deletions (s3:ObjectRemoved) in an S3 bucket can trigger a Lambda function.

- **Common Use Cases**:
1. **Image Processing**:
    - Upload an image to S3, trigger Lambda to resize or add watermarks, and store the processed image in another bucket.
    2. **Log File Analysis**:
        - Automatically process log files uploaded to S3, extract insights, and store results in DynamoDB or another database.

- **Setting Up S3 Integration**:
0. Create an S3 bucket (e.g., file-uploads).
    1. Add an event notification in the S3 bucket settings.
    2. Link the notification to an existing Lambda function or create a new one.

---

2.   Amazon   DynamoDB   and   Lambda

Amazon DynamoDB is a NoSQL database service that integrates seamlessly with Lambda for real-time data handling.

- **How It Works**:
    o DynamoDB Streams capture changes (insert, update, delete) in a table and trigger a Lambda function for processing.
- **Common Use Cases**:
1. **Real-Time Analytics**:

- Monitor product inventory updates and calculate real-time metrics.

2. **Data Synchronization**:
   - Synchronize changes in a DynamoDB table with another system or service.

- **Setting Up DynamoDB Integration**:

0. Enable DynamoDB Streams on your table.

   1. Create a Lambda function to process stream events.
   2. Grant the Lambda function necessary permissions in IAM.

---

3.   Amazon   SNS   and   Lambda

Amazon Simple Notification Service (SNS) enables message broadcasting and notifications, with Lambda acting as a subscriber.

- **How It Works**:
  - SNS topics can trigger Lambda functions upon receiving messages.
- **Common Use Cases**:

1. **Alert Systems**:
   - An application detects an anomaly and sends an alert to SNS, which triggers a Lambda function to log or further process the event.

   2. **Chaining Workflows**:

- A Lambda function publishes a message to an SNS topic, triggering additional functions or notifying users.
- **Setting Up SNS Integration**:

0. Create an SNS topic.
   1. Subscribe a Lambda function to the topic.
   2. Publish a message to the topic to trigger the function.

Building an Event-Driven Workflow

Event-driven workflows allow systems to react dynamically to events, ensuring scalability and responsiveness.

---

1. Workflow Design Principles:

- **Decoupling**:
  o Separate each component to ensure independent scaling and fault isolation.
- **Event Propagation**:
  o Use event-driven services like EventBridge or SQS for smooth message flow.
- **Chaining**:
  o Link multiple Lambda functions together using services like Step Functions or SNS.

2. Sample Workflow: *File Processing Pipeline*

A common event-driven workflow for processing uploaded files in S3.

1. **Scenario**:
   - A user uploads a video to S3.
   - The video is transcoded into multiple formats for playback on different devices.

2. **Workflow Steps**:

1. **File Upload**:
   - User uploads the video to an S3 bucket (raw-videos).

2. **Trigger Lambda**:
   - S3 event notification triggers a Lambda function.

3. **Video Processing**:
   - Lambda sends the video to AWS Elastic Transcoder or MediaConvert.

4. **Post-Processing**:
   - Lambda stores transcoded files in another bucket (processed-videos).

5. **Notification**:
   - Lambda publishes a message to an SNS topic to notify the user.

3.   Workflow   with   Step   Functions

AWS Step Functions orchestrate complex workflows by chaining multiple Lambda functions.

- **Example: Order Processing System**:
    1. **Receive Order**:
        - API Gateway triggers a Lambda function to validate the order.
    2. **Payment Processing**:
        - The first function calls another Lambda function to handle payment.
    3. **Inventory Update**:
        - A final Lambda function updates inventory in DynamoDB.
    4. **Notification**:
        - SNS sends order confirmation to the customer.

Real-World Use Cases for AWS Integrations

1. **Serverless Data Lake**:
    o **Workflow**:
        1. Data is ingested into S3 from various sources (IoT, logs, external systems).

2. A Lambda function processes and categorizes the data.

3. The data is stored in S3 or DynamoDB for analysis.

o **Benefits**: Scalability, low cost, and real-time insights.

2. **E-Commerce Platform**:

o **Workflow**:

1. API Gateway invokes Lambda for managing product catalogs and user orders.

2. Order data is stored in DynamoDB.

3. SNS sends notifications for new orders.

o **Benefits**: Cost efficiency and high availability.

3. **IoT Data Processing**:

o **Workflow**:

1. IoT devices send telemetry data to AWS IoT Core.

2. IoT Core triggers a Lambda function to process the data.

3. Processed data is stored in DynamoDB or analyzed in Amazon QuickSight.

o **Benefits**: Handles high data velocity with low latency.

4. **Customer Support Chatbots**:

o **Workflow**:

1. A chatbot built using Amazon Lex sends user queries to Lambda.
2. Lambda fetches relevant data from DynamoDB.
3. The chatbot responds to the user with the information.

- **Benefits**: Provides automated, 24/7 customer support.

5. **Real-Time Fraud Detection**:
   - **Workflow**:
     1. Transaction data flows into DynamoDB Streams.
     2. A Lambda function evaluates the data against fraud detection rules.
     3. If fraud is detected, Lambda publishes alerts via SNS.
   - **Benefits**: Immediate detection and response to suspicious activities.

Integrating AWS services with Lambda unlocks the full potential of serverless applications. Whether processing files, managing real-time data, or building complex workflows, these integrations provide the tools and scalability needed for modern applications.

With a solid understanding of AWS service triggers and real-world use cases, readers can start designing robust event-driven systems.

Chapter 7: Using the Serverless Framework

The Serverless Framework is a powerful open-source framework that simplifies the deployment and management of serverless applications. This chapter introduces the framework, walks you through setting up and deploying a Lambda function using it, and highlights the real-world benefits of adopting such a tool.

Introduction to the Serverless Framework

1. **What Is the Serverless Framework?**
   - The Serverless Framework is a command-line tool and framework that makes it easier to build and manage serverless applications.
   - It abstracts complex configurations and provides a unified way to work with multiple cloud providers, such as AWS, Azure, and Google Cloud.
2. **Key Features**:
   - **Simplified Deployment**: Write a simple configuration file to define your infrastructure and deploy it with a single command.
   - **Multi-Cloud Support**: Build serverless applications that can run across different cloud providers.

- o **Extensibility**: Supports plugins and custom workflows to adapt to your application's needs.
- o **Monitoring and Debugging**: Integrated tools provide insights into your application's performance and errors.

3. **Why Use the Serverless Framework?**
   - o Reduces the time and effort required to configure and deploy serverless resources.
   - o Provides a consistent structure for managing serverless projects, making collaboration easier.
   - o Enhances scalability with built-in best practices for serverless development.

4. **Real-World Example**:
   - o A startup uses the Serverless Framework to deploy an API backed by AWS Lambda and DynamoDB. With its simple syntax and automated deployment, the team saves hours of manual setup and focuses on building features.

Setting Up and Deploying a Lambda Function

1. **Prerequisites**:
   - o Node.js installed on your system.

- o AWS account credentials with permissions to deploy Lambda functions.
- o The Serverless Framework installed globally via npm:

bash

npm install -g serverless

2. **Creating Your First Serverless Project**:
   - o Initialize a new project:

bash

serverless create --template aws-nodejs --path my-first-service
cd my-first-service

   - o This creates a project with a predefined structure:
     - **handler.js**: Contains the Lambda function code.
     - **serverless.yml**: The configuration file for defining resources and functions.

3. **Writing Your Lambda Function**:
   - o Open handler.js and write a simple function:

javascript

```
module.exports.hello = async (event) => {
    return {
```

```
        statusCode: 200,
        body: JSON.stringify({
            message: "Hello, Serverless Framework!",
        }),
    };
};
```

4. Configuring the Deployment:

- o Edit serverless.yml to define the function:

  yaml

  ```yaml
  service: my-first-service
  provider:
   name: aws
   runtime: nodejs16.x
  functions:
   hello:
    handler: handler.hello
    events:
     - http:
       path: hello
       method: get
  ```

- o Key sections in serverless.yml:

    - **provider**: Specifies the cloud provider and runtime.

    - **functions**: Defines the Lambda functions and their triggers.

- **events**: Defines how the function is triggered, such as via an HTTP request.

5. **Deploying the Function**:
   - o Deploy your function using the Serverless CLI:

   bash

   ```
   serverless deploy
   ```

   - o The framework provisions the necessary AWS resources, including:
     - A Lambda function.
     - An API Gateway endpoint for the HTTP trigger.
   - o After deployment, you'll see an output like this:

   plaintext

   ```
   Service Information
   service: my-first-service
   stage: dev
   region: us-east-1
   endpoint: https://random-api-id.amazonaws.com/dev/hello
   ```

6. **Testing the Function**:
   - o Use the endpoint provided in the output to test the function:

   bash

```
curl https://random-api-id.amazonaws.com/dev/hello
```

- The function responds with:

json

```json
{
    "message": "Hello, Serverless Framework!"
}
```

7. **Updating and Redeploying**:
   - Modify the code or configuration, then redeploy with:

bash

```bash
serverless deploy
```

   - Only the modified parts are redeployed, saving time.

Real-World Benefits of Using Frameworks

1. **Time Efficiency**:
   - Automates repetitive tasks such as setting up infrastructure, deploying functions, and managing updates.

- o Example: A developer deploying an application with multiple Lambda functions saves hours of manual configuration.

2. **Ease of Collaboration**:
   - o Standardized project structure and YAML-based configuration make it easy for teams to collaborate.
   - o Example: New developers can quickly onboard by understanding the serverless.yml configuration.

3. **Simplified Multi-Environment Management**:
   - o Easily manage multiple environments (e.g., dev, staging, prod) with built-in support for stages.
   - o Example:

   bash

   serverless deploy --stage prod

4. **Cost Optimization**:
   - o Integrated monitoring tools help identify inefficiencies in function execution and resource usage.
   - o Example: Analyze CloudWatch metrics directly from the framework to reduce execution time and cost.

5. **Extensibility**:

- o Plugins add additional functionality, such as offline development or custom deployment workflows.
- o Example: The serverless-offline plugin enables local testing of HTTP endpoints without deploying to AWS.

6. **Improved Application Reliability**:
- o Consistent configurations reduce human errors during deployment.
- o Example: Version control ensures that changes to serverless.yml can be tracked and reverted if necessary.

The Serverless Framework is a game-changer for managing serverless applications. By simplifying deployment, standardizing workflows, and integrating with multiple cloud providers, it empowers developers to focus on building applications rather than managing infrastructure. Through practical steps and real-world benefits, this chapter equips readers with the knowledge to get started with the framework and maximize its potential.

Chapter 8: Deploying Lambda Functions with AWS SAM

The AWS Serverless Application Model (SAM) simplifies the process of building, deploying, and managing serverless applications on AWS. This chapter explains what SAM is, walks you through installing and configuring it, and demonstrates how to deploy a sample serverless application.

What is AWS Serverless Application Model (SAM)?

1. **Definition**:
   - AWS SAM is an open-source framework that extends AWS CloudFormation to simplify the definition and deployment of serverless applications.
   - It provides shorthand syntax for defining serverless resources like Lambda functions, API Gateway endpoints, DynamoDB tables, and more.

2. **Key Features**:
   - **Simplified Resource Definition**:
     - SAM uses a simplified template format to define serverless resources.
     - Example:

```yaml
Resources:
  MyFunction:
    Type: AWS::Serverless::Function
    Properties:
      Handler: app.lambda_handler
      Runtime: python3.9
      Events:
        Api:
          Type: Api
          Properties:
            Path: /hello
            Method: get
```

- **Built-In Testing and Debugging**:
  - Use SAM CLI to locally test and debug Lambda functions.
- **Integration with AWS Services**:
  - Seamlessly integrates with API Gateway, DynamoDB, S3, and other AWS services.
- **CI/CD Support**:
  - Automate deployments with AWS CodePipeline or other CI/CD tools.

3. **Benefits of SAM**:
   - **Developer Productivity**: Simplifies complex CloudFormation templates for serverless.

- o **Local Testing**: Test Lambda functions locally, simulating the AWS environment.
- o **Extensibility**: Leverage the power of CloudFormation with additional SAM-specific features.

Installing and Configuring AWS SAM

To use AWS SAM, you need to install the SAM CLI and configure your development environment.

1. **Prerequisites**:
   - o Install the following tools:
     - **AWS CLI**: To interact with AWS services.
     - **Docker**: Required for local testing and building functions.
     - **Node.js**: Needed for some SAM applications (optional based on language).
   - o An AWS account with IAM permissions for deploying serverless resources.
2. **Installing SAM CLI**:
   - o Follow the instructions for your operating system:
     - **macOS**:

       bash

brew install aws/tap/aws-sam-cli

- **Windows**:

  - Download the installer from the AWS SAM CLI website.

- **Linux**:

  bash

  curl -Lo sam-installation.zip
  https://github.com/aws/aws-sam-cli/releases/latest/download/aws-sam-cli-linux-x86_64.zip
  unzip sam-installation.zip -d sam-installation
  sudo ./sam-installation/install

3. **Verifying Installation**:

   o Check if SAM CLI is installed:

   bash

   sam --version

   o Example output:

   objectivec

   SAM CLI, version X.X.X

4. **Configuring AWS Credentials**:

o   Use the AWS CLI to configure credentials:

bash

aws configure

o   Provide:
  ▪   **Access Key ID** and **Secret Access Key**.
  ▪   **Default Region** (e.g., us-east-1).

Deploying a Sample Serverless Application

1. **Step 1: Initialize a New SAM Application**:
   o   Create a new project using a template:

   bash

   sam init

   o   Choose options:
     ▪   **Runtime**: Select your preferred language (e.g., Python 3.9, Node.js 16.x).
     ▪   **Template**: Choose a "Hello World" example.
   o   Navigate to the project directory:

   bash

```
cd sam-app
```

2. **Step 2: Understanding the Project Structure**:

    o   Typical structure of a SAM application:

    bash

    ```
    ├── README.md
    ├── events/          # Example event payloads for testing
    ├── hello_world/       # Lambda function code
    │   ├── app.py          # Your Lambda function handler
    │   └── requirements.txt  # Dependencies (Python example)
    ├── template.yaml       # SAM template
    ```

    o   **template.yaml**:

    - Defines resources (e.g., Lambda functions, API Gateway endpoints).

3. **Step 3: Build the Application**:

    o   Use the SAM CLI to build the application:

    bash

    ```
    sam build
    ```

    o   This step packages your application and dependencies into a deployable format.

4. **Step 4: Test the Application Locally**:

    o   Start the local API:

bash

sam local start-api

o   Use tools like curl or Postman to test endpoints:

bash

curl http://127.0.0.1:3000/hello

o   Example response:

json

```
{
    "message": "Hello, World!"
}
```

5. **Step 5: Deploy the Application**:

   o   Package and deploy the application to AWS:

bash

sam deploy --guided

   o   During the guided deployment, provide:

   ▪   **Stack Name**: A unique name for your application stack.

   ▪   **Region**: AWS region for deployment.

- o SAM generates an S3 bucket for storing deployment artifacts and deploys the application.

6. **Step 6: Verify Deployment**:
   - o After deployment, the CLI displays API Gateway endpoint URLs:

   plaintext

   ```
   Outputs:
   HelloWorldApi:
       Description: API Gateway endpoint URL for Prod stage
       Value: https://random-api-id.amazonaws.com/Prod/hello
   ```

   - o Test the deployed endpoint using curl or a browser:

   bash

   ```
   curl https://random-api-id.amazonaws.com/Prod/hello
   ```

Real-World Applications of AWS SAM

1. **E-Commerce Platform**:
   - o Use SAM to deploy a scalable API for managing orders and product inventory.
   - o Example:
     - Lambda handles order processing.
     - DynamoDB stores inventory data.

- API Gateway exposes RESTful endpoints for frontend applications.

2. **IoT Data Pipeline**:
   o Deploy an event-driven architecture with SAM to process IoT sensor data.
   o Example:
     - IoT Core sends data to an S3 bucket.
     - Lambda functions process the data and store insights in DynamoDB.

3. **Automated Reporting**:
   o Use SAM to automate daily reports.
   o Example:
     - A scheduled EventBridge trigger invokes a Lambda function to analyze S3 data and send reports via SNS.

AWS SAM simplifies the deployment and management of serverless applications, making it an essential tool for developers working with AWS Lambda. By following this chapter's steps, readers can set up their environment, deploy applications, and explore the full potential of SAM in real-world scenarios.

Chapter 9: Building APIs with AWS Lambda and API Gateway

AWS Lambda and API Gateway work seamlessly together to build scalable and efficient RESTful APIs. This chapter explores creating APIs, configuring routes and endpoints, and provides a hands-on example to illustrate the process.

Creating RESTful APIs with Lambda

1. **What Is a RESTful API?**
   - o RESTful APIs follow Representational State Transfer (REST) principles, allowing clients to interact with resources using standard HTTP methods (GET, POST, PUT, DELETE).
   - o Each resource is identified by a unique URL endpoint.

2. **Why Use Lambda for APIs?**
   - o **Serverless**: No server management; pay only for usage.
   - o **Scalability**: Automatically handles millions of requests.
   - o **Flexibility**: Easily integrate with other AWS services.

3. **Lambda's Role in APIs**:

   o Handles the logic for processing API requests.

   o Responds with structured data (e.g., JSON) to clients.

   o Examples:

   - **GET**: Fetch data from DynamoDB.

   - **POST**: Add new items to a database.

   - **DELETE**: Remove an item.

Configuring Routes and Endpoints with API Gateway

API Gateway is the entry point for your RESTful API, connecting HTTP requests to AWS Lambda functions.

1. **Understanding API Gateway Components**:

   o **Resources**: Represents the path of your API endpoint (e.g., /users).

   o **Methods**: HTTP methods supported by the resource (e.g., GET, POST).

   o **Integrations**: Links methods to backend services like Lambda.

2. **Creating a Basic API Gateway**:

   o **Step 1: Create a New API**:

   1. Open the API Gateway Console.

   2. Choose **Create API** and select **HTTP API** or **REST API**.

- o **Step 2: Define Resources**:
    1. Add a resource path (e.g., /users).
- o **Step 3: Attach Methods**:
    1. For each resource, add methods like GET or POST.
- o **Step 4: Integrate with Lambda**:
    1. Choose **Lambda Function** as the integration type.
    2. Specify the name of the Lambda function to invoke.

3. **Deploying the API**:
   - o Deploy your API to a stage (e.g., prod).
   - o API Gateway generates a URL for the deployed API:

   arduino

   https://api-id.amazonaws.com/prod/users

4. **Securing the API**:
   - o Use API Gateway features like IAM authorization, API keys, or Lambda Authorizers to secure endpoints.

Hands-on API Development Example

Let's build a RESTful API to manage a list of tasks.

1. Use Case:

- **GET**: Retrieve all tasks.
- **POST**: Add a new task.

2. Lambda Function Code:

Create a Lambda function named TaskManager.

- **Python Example**:

```python
python

import json

tasks = []

def lambda_handler(event, context):
    method = event['httpMethod']
    if method == 'GET':
        return {
            'statusCode': 200,
            'body': json.dumps(tasks)
        }
    elif method == 'POST':
        body = json.loads(event['body'])
        task = {
```

```
        'id': len(tasks) + 1,
        'title': body['title'],
        'completed': False
    }
    tasks.append(task)
    return {
        'statusCode': 201,
        'body': json.dumps(task)
    }
else:
    return {
        'statusCode': 405,
        'body': json.dumps({'message': 'Method Not Allowed'})
    }
```

3. Setting Up API Gateway:

1. **Create API**:
   - Open the API Gateway console and create a REST API.
   - Name the API TaskAPI.

2. **Define Resources**:
   - Add a resource named /tasks.

3. **Attach Methods**:
   - For /tasks, add two methods:
     - **GET**: Link to the TaskManager Lambda function.

- **POST**: Link to the same Lambda function.

4. **Deploy the API**:
   - o Deploy the API to a stage (e.g., prod).
   - o Note the base URL:

   arduino

   https://api-id.amazonaws.com/prod

---

4. Testing the API:

- **GET Request**:
  - o URL: https://api-id.amazonaws.com/prod/tasks
  - o Method: GET
  - o Response:

  json

  []

- **POST Request**:
  - o URL: https://api-id.amazonaws.com/prod/tasks
  - o Method: POST
  - o Body:

  json

  {

```
    "title": "Learn AWS Lambda"
}
```

o   Response:

json

```
{
  "id": 1,
  "title": "Learn AWS Lambda",
  "completed": false
}
```

- **GET Request After Adding Task**:
  - o   URL: https://api-id.amazonaws.com/prod/tasks
  - o   Method: GET
  - o   Response:

json

```
[
  {
    "id": 1,
    "title": "Learn AWS Lambda",
    "completed": false
  }
]
```

Best Practices for API Development

1. **Use Versioning**:

   o Add version numbers to API paths (e.g., /v1/tasks) to support backward compatibility.

2. **Error Handling**:

   o Return appropriate status codes and error messages for invalid requests.

3. **Secure APIs**:

   o Use authentication mechanisms like IAM roles, JWT tokens, or API keys.

4. **Monitor and Optimize**:

   o Use CloudWatch to monitor API usage, latency, and errors.

   o Optimize Lambda execution time to reduce costs.

By combining AWS Lambda and API Gateway, developers can create scalable, cost-efficient RESTful APIs with minimal effort. This chapter has provided the foundational steps to build and test a basic API, along with best practices for developing robust serverless APIs.

Chapter 10: Managing Data in Serverless Applications

Serverless applications often require robust data management solutions to handle varying data types and workloads. This chapter explores how to choose between relational (RDS) and NoSQL (DynamoDB) databases, interact with these databases using AWS Lambda, and provides practical examples of database integration.

Choosing Between Relational (RDS) and NoSQL (DynamoDB) Databases

The choice of database depends on the application's data structure, scalability requirements, and query complexity.

---

1. Relational Databases (RDS)

- **Overview**:
  - Relational databases store structured data in tables with predefined schemas.
  - Examples: MySQL, PostgreSQL, Microsoft SQL Server, Amazon Aurora (all supported by AWS RDS).
- **Key Features**:

- o Supports SQL for complex queries and transactions.
- o Ideal for applications requiring strong relationships between data (e.g., foreign keys, joins).

- **Use Cases**:
  - o E-commerce systems requiring transaction management.
  - o Applications needing complex reporting and analytics.

- **Pros**:
  - o ACID compliance ensures data consistency.
  - o Suitable for structured, well-defined data.

- **Cons**:
  - o Less flexible for unstructured data.
  - o Scaling horizontally can be challenging compared to NoSQL.

2. NoSQL Databases (DynamoDB)

- **Overview**:
  - o DynamoDB is a fully managed NoSQL database designed for high scalability and low-latency performance.
  - o Data is stored in a key-value or document format.

- **Key Features**:
  - o No predefined schema; flexible data modeling.

- Scales horizontally to handle massive traffic.
- **Use Cases**:
  - Real-time applications (e.g., gaming leaderboards, IoT data ingestion).
  - Applications requiring high throughput and low latency.
- **Pros**:
  - Automatically scales based on workload.
  - Cost-efficient for large-scale data storage.
- **Cons**:
  - Limited support for complex queries (e.g., joins, subqueries).
  - Querying requires knowledge of data access patterns.

3. Comparing RDS and DynamoDB

Feature	RDS	DynamoDB
Schema	Fixed schema	Schema-less
Query Language	SQL	Key-value and indexes
Scalability	Vertical or read replicas	Horizontal (automatic)

Feature	RDS	DynamoDB
Transactions	ACID-compliant	ACID for single-partition
Cost	Fixed instance pricing	Pay-per-use

Using Lambda to Interact with Databases

AWS Lambda can act as a bridge between your application and your chosen database.

1. Interacting with RDS

- **Setting Up RDS**:
    1. Create an RDS instance in the AWS Management Console.
    2. Configure security groups to allow connections from Lambda.
    3. Store credentials securely using AWS Secrets Manager or environment variables.
- **Lambda Code Example**:
    o **Python with MySQL**:

        python

```python
import pymysql
import json

def lambda_handler(event, context):
    connection = pymysql.connect(
        host="your-rds-endpoint",
        user="your-username",
        password="your-password",
        database="your-database"
    )
    cursor = connection.cursor()
    cursor.execute("SELECT * FROM users")
    rows = cursor.fetchall()
    connection.close()

    return {
        'statusCode': 200,
        'body': json.dumps(rows)
    }
```

- **Best Practices**:
  - o Use connection pooling libraries like mysql-connector-python to optimize database connections.
  - o Minimize open connections by closing them immediately after use.

2. Interacting with DynamoDB

- **Setting Up DynamoDB**:
  1. Create a DynamoDB table and define primary keys.
  2. Grant Lambda permissions to interact with the table via an IAM role.
- **Lambda Code Example**:
  - **Python with Boto3**:

```python
python

import boto3
import json

dynamodb = boto3.resource('dynamodb')
table = dynamodb.Table('Tasks')

def lambda_handler(event, context):
    # Adding a new item
    item = {
        'TaskID': '1',
        'Title': 'Learn AWS Lambda',
        'Completed': False
    }
    table.put_item(Item=item)

    # Fetching all items
    response = table.scan()
    return {
        'statusCode': 200,
        'body': json.dumps(response['Items'])
```

```
}
```

- **Best Practices**:
  - o Use query or get operations over scan for better performance.
  - o Optimize partition keys and indexes for predictable access patterns.

Practical Examples of Database Integration

1. **Example 1: User Management System with RDS**
   - o **Use Case**: An API for managing user profiles.
   - o **Workflow**:
     1. A Lambda function handles HTTP requests from API Gateway.
     2. For a GET request, the function fetches user details from an RDS MySQL database.
   - o **Code Snippet**:

   python

   ```python
   cursor.execute("SELECT * FROM users WHERE user_id = %s", (event['pathParameters']['id'],))
   ```

---

2. **Example 2: Real-Time Leaderboard with DynamoDB**

- o **Use Case**: A gaming application requires a leaderboard updated in real-time.
- o **Workflow**:
    1. Players submit scores through an API.
    2. A Lambda function updates the score in DynamoDB.
    3. The leaderboard is retrieved with sorted queries.
- o **Code Snippet**:

python

```python
response = table.query(
    IndexName='ScoreIndex',
    KeyConditionExpression=Key('GameID').eq('1'),
    ScanIndexForward=False  # Descending order
)
```

3. **Example 3: E-Commerce Inventory Management**
    - o **Use Case**: An inventory system tracks stock levels.
    - o **Workflow**:
        1. Orders placed via API Gateway invoke a Lambda function.
        2. The function updates stock levels in DynamoDB.

3. If stock is low, Lambda triggers an SNS notification.

- **Code Snippet**:

python

```
table.update_item(
    Key={'ProductID': '123'},
    UpdateExpression="SET Stock = Stock - :qty",
    ExpressionAttributeValues={':qty': 1}
)
```

Effective data management is key to building powerful serverless applications. Whether using RDS for complex relational data or DynamoDB for high-performance NoSQL storage, AWS Lambda provides seamless integration. By understanding the strengths of each database type and following best practices, developers can design scalable and efficient data-driven solutions.

Chapter 11: Securing Your Serverless Applications

Security is paramount when building serverless applications, as they are often exposed to external access points like APIs and integrate with critical resources. This chapter focuses on implementing IAM roles and policies, securing APIs with API Gateway and Lambda Authorizers, and outlines best practices for securing serverless architectures.

Implementing IAM Roles and Policies

AWS Identity and Access Management (IAM) is central to securing serverless applications by defining fine-grained access controls.

---

1. What Are IAM Roles and Policies?

- **IAM Roles**:
  - Allow AWS services like Lambda to interact with other AWS resources securely.
  - Example: A Lambda function using a role to read from an S3 bucket or query a DynamoDB table.
- **IAM Policies**:

- JSON documents that define permissions for IAM roles.
- Example: A policy granting s3:GetObject access to a specific S3 bucket.

---

2. Setting Up IAM Roles for Lambda

- **Creating an IAM Role**:
    1. Open the **IAM Console** and create a role.
    2. Choose **AWS Service** as the trusted entity and select **Lambda**.
    3. Attach the necessary policies (e.g., AmazonS3ReadOnlyAccess).
    4. Name and save the role.
- **Assigning the Role to a Lambda Function**:
    1. Navigate to the Lambda function in the AWS Management Console.
    2. Under the **Configuration** tab, select **Permissions**.
    3. Edit the execution role and attach the newly created role.

---

3. Examples of IAM Policies

- **Minimal Policy for DynamoDB Access**:

json

```json
{
  "Version": "2012-10-17",
  "Statement": [
    {
      "Effect": "Allow",
      "Action": [
        "dynamodb:GetItem",
        "dynamodb:PutItem"
      ],
      "Resource":                          "arn:aws:dynamodb:us-east-1:123456789012:table/MyTable"
    }
  ]
}
```

- **Policy for S3 Read/Write Access**:

json

```json
{
  "Version": "2012-10-17",
  "Statement": [
    {
      "Effect": "Allow",
      "Action": [
        "s3:GetObject",
        "s3:PutObject"
      ],
```

```
          "Resource": "arn:aws:s3:::my-bucket/*"
      }
    ]
  }
```

Securing APIs with API Gateway and Lambda Authorizers

APIs are often the entry point to serverless applications, making their security critical.

1. Using API Gateway to Secure APIs

- **Enabling HTTPS**:
    - API Gateway enforces HTTPS connections by default, ensuring data is encrypted in transit.
- **Using API Keys**:
    - Require clients to include an API key in requests.
    - Limit the access and monitor usage of each key.
- **Throttling and Rate Limiting**:
    - Configure usage plans to limit the number of requests per second, protecting APIs from abuse or DDoS attacks.

2. Lambda Authorizers

- **What Is a Lambda Authorizer?**
  - A Lambda function that authenticates and authorizes API requests before invoking the backend function.
  - Example: Validate a JSON Web Token (JWT) or an OAuth token.

- **Types of Lambda Authorizers**:
  - **Token-Based**: Validates tokens passed in the Authorization header.
  - **Request Parameter-Based**: Evaluates query parameters or headers.

- **Example of a Token-Based Lambda Authorizer (Node.js)**:

javascript

```javascript
exports.handler = async (event) => {
  const token = event.authorizationToken;
  if (token === "valid-token") {
    return {
      principalId: "user123",
      policyDocument: {
        Version: "2012-10-17",
        Statement: [
          {
            Action: "execute-api:Invoke",
            Effect: "Allow",
            Resource: event.methodArn
          }
```

```
        ]
      }
    };
  } else {
    throw new Error("Unauthorized");
  }
};
```

- **Configuring a Lambda Authorizer**:
1. In the API Gateway Console, select your API.
    2. Under **Authorizers**, add a new Lambda Authorizer.
    3. Link it to the Lambda function and specify the token source (e.g., Authorization header).
    4. Apply the authorizer to API methods (e.g., GET, POST).

Best Practices for Securing Serverless Architectures

1. **Follow the Principle of Least Privilege**:
    o Grant only the permissions necessary for a function to operate.
    o Regularly review and update IAM roles and policies.
2. **Secure Sensitive Data**:
    o Use AWS Secrets Manager or Parameter Store to store sensitive information (e.g., database credentials, API keys).

o Example: Pass a database password securely as an environment variable using Secrets Manager.

3. **Enable Encryption**:

   o **In Transit**: Ensure HTTPS is used for all API Gateway requests.

   o **At Rest**: Encrypt data in S3 buckets and DynamoDB tables.

4. **Monitor and Log Activity**:

   o Enable CloudWatch Logs for Lambda to monitor execution.

   o Use AWS CloudTrail to track API calls and detect suspicious activity.

5. **Set Up Alarms and Alerts**:

   o Use CloudWatch Alarms to notify you of unusual activity, such as spikes in Lambda invocations or errors.

6. **Validate Input**:

   o Sanitize and validate all user inputs to prevent injection attacks (e.g., SQL injection, XSS).

7. **Limit Function Execution Time**:

   o Set reasonable timeouts for Lambda functions to avoid prolonged execution due to abuse or errors.

8. **Use VPC for Sensitive Data**:

   o Deploy Lambda functions inside a VPC if they need access to private resources, such as RDS instances.

9. **Regularly Update Dependencies**:
   o Keep Lambda packages and dependencies up to date to patch security vulnerabilities.

10. **Audit Permissions Regularly**:
    o Periodically review IAM roles and policies to ensure they align with security standards.

Securing serverless applications requires a combination of fine-grained access control, secure data handling, and proactive monitoring. By implementing IAM roles and policies, securing APIs with Lambda Authorizers, and adhering to best practices, you can build serverless architectures that are both robust and resilient to attacks.

Chapter 12: Error Handling and Debugging Lambda Functions

Error handling and debugging are critical to maintaining reliable serverless applications. This chapter delves into AWS Lambda error types, using AWS CloudWatch for logging and monitoring, and real-world techniques for debugging Lambda functions.

Understanding AWS Lambda Error Types

AWS Lambda functions can encounter several error types during execution. Understanding these errors is crucial for implementing robust error handling strategies.

---

1. Invocation Errors

- **Definition**: Errors that occur when AWS Lambda fails to invoke a function.
- **Common Causes**:
    o   Incorrect IAM permissions.
    o   Misconfigured triggers (e.g., API Gateway or S3).
    o   Exceeding concurrency limits.
- **Example**:

o   An API Gateway trigger lacks the necessary permissions to invoke a Lambda function.

---

2. Runtime Errors

- **Definition**: Errors that occur during the execution of a Lambda function.
- **Common Causes**:
    o   Syntax errors in the code.
    o   Missing environment variables.
    o   Invalid function logic (e.g., division by zero).
- **Example**:
    o   A Python function with a KeyError when accessing a nonexistent key in a dictionary.

---

3. Timeout Errors

- **Definition**: Errors that occur when a Lambda function exceeds its execution timeout.
- **Common Causes**:
    o   Long-running operations such as database queries or API calls.
    o   Infinite loops in the code.
- **Example**:

o A function fetching data from an external API with slow response times exceeds the default 3-second timeout.

---

4. Resource Errors

- **Definition**: Errors caused by exceeding allocated resources.
- **Common Causes**:
    o Insufficient memory allocation.
    o Hitting AWS service quotas (e.g., DynamoDB read/write capacity).
- **Example**:
    o A Lambda function with insufficient memory fails while processing a large file.

---

5. Permissions Errors

- **Definition**: Errors resulting from misconfigured IAM policies or roles.
- **Common Causes**:
    o Function lacks permission to access an S3 bucket or DynamoDB table.
- **Example**:

- A function attempting to read from an S3 bucket without the s3:GetObject permission.

Using AWS CloudWatch for Logging and Monitoring

AWS CloudWatch is a powerful tool for monitoring and debugging Lambda functions.

---

1. Enabling CloudWatch Logs

- **Default Behavior**:
  - Lambda automatically streams logs to CloudWatch for every invocation.
  - Each log stream corresponds to a specific instance of a function.
- **Custom Logging**:
  - Use logging libraries (e.g., console.log in Node.js or print in Python) to output custom logs.
  - Example (Python):

  python

  import logging

  logger = logging.getLogger()
  logger.setLevel(logging.INFO)

```
def lambda_handler(event, context):
    logger.info("Event received: %s", event)
    return {"statusCode": 200, "body": "Hello, World!"}
```

2. Analyzing Logs in CloudWatch

- **Viewing Logs**:

  1. Open the **CloudWatch Console**.

  2. Navigate to **Log Groups** and find the group for your Lambda function (/aws/lambda/<function-name>).

  3. Select a log stream to view execution details.

- **Key Metrics**:

  o **Duration**: Execution time for each invocation.

  o **Billed Duration**: The time for which you are charged.

  o **Errors**: Number of invocations that resulted in errors.

  o **Throttles**: Number of invocations that were throttled due to exceeding concurrency limits.

- **Example Log Entry**:

mathematica

```
START RequestId: 12345678 Version: $LATEST
Event received: {"key": "value"}
END RequestId: 12345678
REPORT RequestId: 12345678 Duration: 123 ms Billed Duration: 200
ms Memory Size: 128 MB Max Memory Used: 56 MB
```

3. Setting Up Alarms for Monitoring

- Use CloudWatch Alarms to monitor metrics and notify you of issues.
    - Example: Create an alarm for the **Error** metric to trigger an SNS notification if errors exceed a certain threshold.

Real-World Debugging Techniques

Debugging serverless applications requires a combination of tools and strategies.

1. Local Testing

- **AWS SAM CLI**:
    - Test Lambda functions locally with the AWS Serverless Application Model (SAM) CLI.
    - Example:

    bash

    ```
    sam local invoke "FunctionName" -e event.json
    ```

- **Mock Events**:
  - o Use sample events to simulate triggers (e.g., S3 uploads, API Gateway requests).

---

2. Structured Logging

- Use structured logging formats (e.g., JSON) to make logs easier to parse and analyze.
- Example:

python

```python
import json
import logging

logger = logging.getLogger()
logger.setLevel(logging.INFO)

def lambda_handler(event, context):
    logger.info(json.dumps({"message": "Processing event", "event": event}))
    return {"statusCode": 200, "body": "Success"}
```

---

3. Layered Debugging

- Break down complex functions into smaller, testable components.

- Test each layer independently to isolate issues.

---

4. AWS X-Ray for Tracing

- **What Is AWS X-Ray?**:
  - A tool for tracing requests through serverless architectures.
  - Identifies latency bottlenecks and errors in distributed systems.
- **Enabling X-Ray**:
1. Enable X-Ray in the Lambda function configuration.
   2. Add the X-Ray SDK to your function code.
- **Example (Python)**:

python

```python
from aws_xray_sdk.core import xray_recorder
from aws_xray_sdk.core import patch_all

patch_all()

def lambda_handler(event, context):
    segment = xray_recorder.begin_segment('LambdaExample')
    # Your function logic here
    xray_recorder.end_segment()
    return {"statusCode": 200, "body": "Traced"}
```

5. Iterative Deployment and Testing

- Deploy functions to a **staging environment** before production.
- Use versioning and aliases to test new versions without affecting live traffic.

---

6. Common Debugging Scenarios

- **Scenario 1**: Function Exceeds Timeout
  - **Issue**: A function fetching data from an external API times out.
  - **Solution**:
    - Increase the timeout limit in the Lambda configuration.
    - Optimize API calls using retries or pagination.
- **Scenario 2**: Insufficient IAM Permissions
  - **Issue**: A function fails to write to an S3 bucket.
  - **Solution**:
    - Add the s3:PutObject permission to the function's IAM role.
- **Scenario 3**: Resource Exhaustion
  - **Issue**: A function processing large files runs out of memory.

o **Solution**:

- Increase the memory allocation in the Lambda configuration.
- Process the file in smaller chunks.

Error handling and debugging are essential to ensuring the reliability of serverless applications. By understanding error types, leveraging tools like CloudWatch and X-Ray, and employing real-world debugging techniques, developers can quickly identify and resolve issues in their AWS Lambda functions.

Chapter 13: Monitoring and Performance Optimization

Monitoring and performance optimization are crucial for ensuring the reliability, scalability, and cost-efficiency of serverless applications. This chapter explores key metrics to monitor, tools like CloudWatch and X-Ray, and provides actionable tips for optimizing AWS Lambda function performance.

Metrics to Monitor in Serverless Applications

Monitoring metrics help track the health and performance of serverless applications. AWS provides several built-in metrics for Lambda, accessible via Amazon CloudWatch.

---

1. Core Metrics for AWS Lambda

Metric	Description
Invocations	Number of times a function is invoked.
Duration	Time taken for a function to execute.
Errors	Number of invocation errors.

Metric	Description
Throttles	Number of throttled invocations due to concurrency limits.
Concurrent Executions	Number of function instances running simultaneously.
Cold Starts	Occurrences of new execution environments being initialized for the function.

2. API Gateway Metrics

For APIs backed by Lambda, monitor the following:

Metric	Description
4XXError	Client-side errors (e.g., bad requests).
5XXError	Server-side errors (e.g., Lambda or API Gateway failures).
Latency	Time taken for API Gateway to process and respond to a request.

3. DynamoDB Metrics (for integrated apps)

Metric	Description
Read/Write Capacity	Tracks the throughput consumed by the application.
Throttled Requests	Number of requests exceeding provisioned capacity.

Tools for Monitoring and Debugging

AWS offers powerful tools like CloudWatch and X-Ray for monitoring and debugging serverless applications.

---

1. Amazon CloudWatch

- **Purpose**:
    - Tracks metrics, collects logs, and sets up alarms for Lambda functions and other AWS services.
- **Key Features**:
    - **Metrics**: Visualize function performance (e.g., duration, errors).
    - **Logs**: View execution details, errors, and custom log messages.
    - **Alarms**: Notify users of performance issues or anomalies.

- **Using CloudWatch Logs Insights**:
  - Query logs to identify trends and issues:

    sql

    ```
    fields @timestamp, @message
    | sort @timestamp desc
    | filter @message like /ERROR/
    ```

  - Example Use Case:
    - Detect repeated invocation errors to debug failing requests.

---

2. AWS X-Ray

- **Purpose**:
  - Provides distributed tracing for serverless applications, helping identify bottlenecks and performance issues.
- **Key Features**:
  - **Service Map**: Visual representation of application components and their interactions.
  - **Traces**: Detailed information about individual requests.
  - **Segments and Subsegments**: Breakdown of execution time for Lambda and integrated services.

- **Enabling X-Ray for Lambda**:

1.   Enable X-Ray tracing in the Lambda function configuration.

    2.   Add the X-Ray SDK to the function code for detailed insights.

- **Real-World Example**:
  - o   Trace an API request to pinpoint latency in database interactions or external API calls.

Tips for Optimizing Lambda Function Performance

Performance optimization ensures functions execute quickly, efficiently, and cost-effectively.

---

1. Optimize Cold Starts

- **What Are Cold Starts?**
  - o   When a Lambda function is invoked after a period of inactivity, AWS initializes a new execution environment, leading to a delay.
- **Mitigation Strategies**:
  - o   **Provisioned Concurrency**:
    - ▪   Pre-warm execution environments to reduce cold start latency.
  - o   **Lightweight Packages**:

BUILDING SERVERLESS APPLICATIONS WITH AWS LAMBDA

- Minimize function size by excluding unnecessary libraries or dependencies.

o **Runtime Selection**:
- Use faster runtimes like Node.js or Python for latency-sensitive applications.

---

2. Reduce Function Execution Time

- **Efficient Code**:
  o Use optimized algorithms and avoid redundant operations.
  o Example: Fetch only required fields from a database rather than entire records.
- **Parallel Processing**:
  o Split tasks into smaller subtasks and execute them concurrently using multiple Lambda functions.
- **Use Caching**:
  o Integrate with services like **Amazon ElastiCache** or **AWS Lambda Extensions** for frequently accessed data.

---

3. Optimize Resource Allocation

- **Memory and CPU Tuning**:

- o Lambda's memory allocation determines the CPU available to a function.
- o Gradually increase memory allocation to improve performance for compute-intensive tasks.
- **Monitor Cost Efficiency**:
  - o Balance resource usage against execution cost to avoid over-provisioning.

---

4. Use Event Filtering

- **Why Filter Events?**
  - o Avoid processing irrelevant events to reduce unnecessary function invocations.
- **Example**:
  - o For an S3 bucket trigger, configure event rules to invoke Lambda only for specific file types.

---

5. Leverage Asynchronous Invocation

- **Purpose**:
  - o For non-critical tasks, use asynchronous invocations to reduce user-facing latency.
- **Example**:

- A Lambda function processes uploaded files asynchronously after an HTTP request is acknowledged.

---

6. Monitor and Improve Database Interactions

- **Batch Processing**:
  - Batch database operations to minimize the number of requests.
- **Efficient Query Design**:
  - Use DynamoDB indexes or optimized SQL queries to reduce query time.

---

7. Automate with Tools

- **Cost Explorer**:
  - Identify cost drivers and optimize Lambda configurations accordingly.
- **Third-Party Tools**:
  - Use tools like Dashbird or Lumigo for advanced monitoring and performance tuning.

Real-World Example: Optimizing an API

Scenario:

An e-commerce application experiences latency in its product catalog API.

Steps Taken:

1. **Analysis**:
   o CloudWatch reveals that database queries are the bottleneck.
   o X-Ray traces show high latency for specific queries.

2. **Optimization**:
   o Added a DynamoDB Global Secondary Index (GSI) to optimize query performance.
   o Increased Lambda memory allocation for faster execution.
   o Enabled Provisioned Concurrency to eliminate cold starts during peak hours.

3. **Results**:
   o API response times improved by 40%.
   o Reduced error rate due to fewer timeouts.

Monitoring and performance optimization are essential to building reliable, cost-efficient serverless applications. By tracking key metrics, leveraging tools like CloudWatch and X-Ray, and applying optimization strategies, developers can ensure their Lambda functions deliver the best possible performance.

Chapter 14: Scaling Serverless Applications

Serverless applications inherently benefit from scalability, with AWS Lambda managing much of the complexity. This chapter explores how AWS Lambda scales automatically, addresses concurrency and throttling limits, and provides real-world examples of scaling serverless applications effectively.

How AWS Lambda Scales Automatically

AWS Lambda is designed to scale horizontally in response to incoming requests. Here's how it works:

---

1. Automatic Scaling Process

- **Event-Based Scaling**:
    - AWS Lambda creates new instances of your function as requests increase.
    - Each instance handles a single request, ensuring isolation and scalability.
- **Concurrent Execution**:
    - When multiple requests arrive, Lambda scales by running multiple concurrent instances of the function.

- o Example:
    - If 100 requests arrive simultaneously, Lambda creates up to 100 instances to handle them.
- **Scaling Duration**:
    - o Instances are created within milliseconds, enabling rapid responses to spikes in demand.

2. Supported Event Sources and Scaling

Event Source	Scaling Behavior
API Gateway	Creates an instance for each request, scaling as demand increases.
S3	Scales based on the number of objects uploaded.
DynamoDB Streams	Scales in proportion to the stream's read throughput.
SQS	Processes messages in batches, scaling with the size of the message queue.

3. Benefits of AWS Lambda's Automatic Scaling

- **Elasticity**:

- Functions scale seamlessly without manual intervention.

- **Cost Efficiency**:
  - Charges are based on the number of requests and execution time, with no idle costs.
- **Resilience**:
  - Handles high traffic volumes and bursts without performance degradation.

Handling Concurrency and Throttling Limits

While AWS Lambda scales automatically, understanding concurrency and throttling limits is essential to prevent performance bottlenecks.

---

1. What Is Concurrency?

- **Definition**:
  - Concurrency refers to the number of function instances running at the same time.
- **Default Concurrency Limit**:
  - By default, each AWS account has a limit of 1,000 concurrent executions per region.

---

2. Throttling

- **What Is Throttling?**
  - Throttling occurs when the number of concurrent executions exceeds the configured limit.
  - Throttled requests are queued or result in 429 Too Many Requests errors.
- **Avoiding Throttling**:
  - Monitor function concurrency using CloudWatch.
  - Increase concurrency limits if necessary.

---

3. Reserved Concurrency

- **Purpose**:
  - Allocate a portion of the concurrency limit exclusively to specific functions.
- **Use Case**:
  - Reserve concurrency for critical functions to ensure availability during high traffic.
- **How to Configure**:
  - In the Lambda function settings, set the desired reserved concurrency value.

---

4. Provisioned Concurrency

- **What Is Provisioned Concurrency?**
  - o Keeps Lambda function instances warm and ready to handle requests, reducing cold start latency.
- **Use Case**:
  - o Critical applications with predictable traffic patterns (e.g., e-commerce checkout systems).
- **How to Enable**:
  - o Configure provisioned concurrency in the Lambda function settings.

---

5. Managing Burst Traffic

- **Initial Burst Capacity**:
  - o AWS Lambda can handle an initial burst of requests per region:
    - Up to 3,000 requests for API Gateway.
    - Up to 1,000 requests for other triggers like S3 or DynamoDB.
- **Sustained Traffic**:
  - o After the burst, Lambda scales at a steady rate (e.g., 500 additional instances per minute).

Real-World Scenarios for Scaling Serverless Applications

Scaling serverless applications is straightforward with AWS Lambda, but strategic planning ensures optimal performance and cost-efficiency.

---

1. Real-Time File Processing

- **Scenario**:
    - A video-sharing platform processes uploaded videos in real time.
- **Solution**:
    - Use S3 to trigger Lambda for each uploaded file.
    - Scale dynamically based on the number of concurrent uploads.
- **Considerations**:
    - Use DynamoDB or SQS to queue metadata for further processing.

---

2. E-Commerce Platform

- **Scenario**:
    - An e-commerce site experiences traffic spikes during flash sales.
- **Solution**:

- o   Use API Gateway to invoke Lambda for order processing.
- o   Enable provisioned concurrency for checkout functions to handle predictable surges.

- **Considerations**:
  - o   Monitor CloudWatch metrics to ensure latency and error rates remain low.

---

3. IoT Data Ingestion

- **Scenario**:
  - o   An IoT system receives data from millions of devices.
- **Solution**:
  - o   Use IoT Core to process incoming data streams.
  - o   Configure Lambda to process batches of data from Kinesis or DynamoDB Streams.
- **Considerations**:
  - o   Optimize batch size to balance processing time and resource usage.

---

4. Chat Application

- **Scenario**:

- o A chat application requires real-time message processing and delivery.

- **Solution**:
  - o Use WebSocket APIs via API Gateway to trigger Lambda for message handling.
  - o Scale dynamically based on active user connections.

- **Considerations**:
  - o Implement rate limiting to prevent abuse and throttling.

---

5. Event-Driven Workflow

- **Scenario**:
  - o A data pipeline processes customer data for analytics.

- **Solution**:
  - o Trigger Lambda using EventBridge for each data source update.
  - o Use Step Functions to orchestrate complex workflows.

- **Considerations**:
  - o Ensure idempotency to handle retries without duplicate processing.

Best Practices for Scaling Serverless Applications

1. **Use Asynchronous Invocations**:
   o For non-critical tasks, use asynchronous invocations to reduce user-facing latency.

2. **Optimize Function Performance**:
   o Minimize execution time by optimizing code and using efficient algorithms.

3. **Leverage Event Filters**:
   o Filter events at the source to avoid unnecessary function invocations.

4. **Monitor Metrics and Set Alarms**:
   o Use CloudWatch to track invocations, errors, and throttling.
   o Set up alarms to notify you of anomalies.

5. **Design for Scalability**:
   o Decouple components using SQS, SNS, or EventBridge.
   o Avoid stateful operations within Lambda functions.

6. **Optimize Costs**:
   o Evaluate memory allocation and execution time to balance performance and cost.

AWS Lambda's automatic scaling capabilities make it a powerful tool for handling diverse workloads. By understanding concurrency limits, leveraging tools like provisioned concurrency, and applying best practices, you can design scalable serverless applications that meet the demands of real-world scenarios.

Chapter 15: Using Step Functions for Orchestrating Workflows

AWS Step Functions enable developers to design and orchestrate complex workflows for serverless applications, ensuring scalability, reliability, and ease of management. This chapter introduces AWS Step Functions, explains how to create and manage workflows, and provides real-world examples of workflow orchestration.

Introduction to AWS Step Functions

AWS Step Functions is a serverless orchestration service that allows developers to coordinate multiple AWS services into automated workflows.

---

1. Key Features of AWS Step Functions

- **Visual Workflow Designer**:
    - Provides a visual representation of workflows, making them easier to design and debug.
- **State Machines**:
    - Workflows in Step Functions are defined as state machines, where each step is a state.
- **Error Handling and Retry**:

- o Automatically handles errors with retry logic, ensuring workflows are robust.
- **Integration with AWS Services**:
  - o Directly integrates with services like AWS Lambda, S3, DynamoDB, and more.
- **Asynchronous and Synchronous Execution**:
  - o Supports long-running workflows, making it ideal for processes like data pipelines.

2. Types of Step Functions Workflows

- **Standard Workflows**:
  - o Designed for long-running or complex workflows with detailed execution history.
  - o Use Cases: Data processing pipelines, multi-step business processes.
- **Express Workflows**:
  - o Designed for high-volume and short-duration workflows.
  - o Use Cases: Real-time data processing, event-driven applications.

3. Benefits of AWS Step Functions

- **Decoupling**:
  - o Separates logic into modular steps, improving maintainability.
- **Scalability**:
  - o Handles complex workflows without requiring manual scaling.
- **Cost Efficiency**:
  - o Pay only for state transitions, making it cost-effective for large workflows.
- **Built-In Resilience**:
  - o Automatically retries failed steps, reducing the risk of workflow interruptions.

Creating and Managing Workflows

---

1. Defining a State Machine

Workflows in Step Functions are defined using the Amazon States Language (ASL), a JSON-based syntax.

Example **Workflow**:

A simple state machine that invokes a Lambda function.

json

```
{
  "Comment": "A simple AWS Step Functions example",
  "StartAt": "InvokeLambda",
  "States": {
   "InvokeLambda": {
    "Type": "Task",
    "Resource":                              "arn:aws:lambda:us-east-
1:123456789012:function:MyLambdaFunction",
    "End": true
   }
  }
}
```

2. Creating a State Machine in the AWS Console

1. **Navigate to Step Functions**:
   o Open the AWS Management Console and go to **Step Functions**.

2. **Create a State Machine**:
   o Select **Standard Workflow** or **Express Workflow**.
   o Define the workflow using the visual editor or import a JSON definition.

3. **Configure Permissions**:
   o Ensure the state machine has permissions to invoke AWS services using an IAM role.

4. **Deploy and Test**:

o   Deploy the state machine and trigger an execution to validate its behavior.

---

3. Managing Workflows

- **Execution Monitoring**:
    - o   View execution history, including input/output data and state transitions.
- **Debugging**:
    - o   Use visual diagrams to identify and troubleshoot errors in the workflow.
- **Versioning and Updates**:
    - o   Update workflows safely by creating new versions or aliases.

Real-World Workflow Orchestration Examples

---

1. Data Processing Pipeline

- **Scenario**:
    - o   An IoT system processes sensor data collected in real time.
- **Workflow**:

1. **Step 1**: Trigger workflow when data is uploaded to S3.

2. **Step 2**: Invoke a Lambda function to process the raw data.

3. **Step 3**: Store the processed data in DynamoDB.

4. **Step 4**: Notify a user via SNS.

- **Benefits**:
  - Ensures data is processed, stored, and notified reliably.

---

2. E-Commerce Order Processing

- **Scenario**:
  - An online store processes customer orders, including payment validation, inventory updates, and notifications.

- **Workflow**:
  1. **Step 1**: Validate order details and check for fraud.
  2. **Step 2**: Process payment using a third-party API.
  3. **Step 3**: Update inventory in DynamoDB.
  4. **Step 4**: Send order confirmation to the customer via email (SES).

- **Benefits**:
  - Orchestrates multiple tasks while handling retries and errors gracefully.

3. Video Processing Pipeline

- **Scenario**:
  - o A video streaming platform processes uploaded videos for multiple formats.
- **Workflow**:
  1. **Step 1**: Trigger workflow on video upload to S3.
  2. **Step 2**: Invoke AWS Elastic Transcoder to create different video formats.
  3. **Step 3**: Store transcoded videos in S3 and update metadata in DynamoDB.
  4. **Step 4**: Notify the user when processing is complete.
- **Benefits**:
  - o Automates a complex pipeline with seamless scaling.

4. Healthcare Data Workflow

- **Scenario**:
  - o A healthcare provider processes patient records from multiple sources.
- **Workflow**:
  1. **Step 1**: Receive data from multiple sources via EventBridge.

2. **Step 2**: Validate and normalize data using Lambda functions.

3. **Step 3**: Store validated data in an RDS instance.

4. **Step 4**: Generate and send reports to doctors via email.

- **Benefits**:

  o Ensures data integrity and compliance with healthcare standards.

---

5. Fraud Detection System

- **Scenario**:

  o A financial system detects and responds to fraudulent activities.

- **Workflow**:

  1. **Step 1**: Analyze transactions using a Lambda function.

  2. **Step 2**: Flag suspicious transactions and log them in DynamoDB.

  3. **Step 3**: Notify the fraud detection team via SNS.

- **Benefits**:

  o Real-time fraud detection with minimal downtime.

Best Practices for Workflow Orchestration

1. **Modular Design**:
   o Break workflows into small, reusable steps for better maintainability.

2. **Error Handling**:
   o Use retry policies and fallback states for robust error handling.

3. **Input/Output Management**:
   o Define clear input and output schemas for each step to avoid data mismatches.

4. **Cost Management**:
   o Optimize the number of state transitions to reduce costs.

5. **Monitor and Debug**:
   o Leverage execution history and CloudWatch Logs for monitoring and debugging workflows.

AWS Step Functions provide a powerful framework for orchestrating complex workflows in serverless applications. By integrating multiple AWS services, handling errors gracefully, and offering visual insights into workflow executions, Step Functions simplify the process of managing automated workflows at scale.

Chapter 16: Building Event-Driven Architectures

Event-driven architectures are a cornerstone of modern, scalable serverless applications. They enable systems to respond to events in real time, promoting decoupling, flexibility, and scalability. This chapter explores the principles of event-driven design, provides examples using AWS services like SQS, SNS, and EventBridge, and showcases practical applications of event-driven patterns.

Event-Driven Design Principles

Event-driven architectures rely on the generation, detection, and reaction to events.

---

1. Core Concepts of Event-Driven Design

- **Event Producers**:
    - Generate events based on actions or changes in the system.
    - Example: An IoT sensor sending temperature data.
- **Event Consumers**:
    - React to events and execute tasks.

- o Example: A Lambda function processing a new record in DynamoDB.
- **Event Brokers**:
  - o Handle the transmission of events between producers and consumers.
  - o Example: SQS queues or EventBridge event buses.

---

2. Characteristics of Event-Driven Architectures

- **Asynchronous Communication**:
  - o Producers and consumers operate independently, reducing tight coupling.
- **Scalability**:
  - o Event-driven systems can scale dynamically with event volumes.
- **Resilience**:
  - o Built-in retry mechanisms and fault tolerance improve reliability.
- **Loose Coupling**:
  - o Components interact through events, minimizing dependencies.

---

3. Types of Events

- **Notification Events**:
  - o Inform consumers about changes without expecting a response.
  - o Example: An SNS topic notifying subscribers of new data.
- **Data Events**:
  - o Contain payloads for processing.
  - o Example: An S3 ObjectCreated event with file metadata.
- **Command Events**:
  - o Direct consumers to perform specific actions.
  - o Example: A message in SQS instructing a Lambda function to resize an image.

Examples Using SQS, SNS, and EventBridge

AWS provides several services for implementing event-driven architectures.

---

1. Amazon Simple Queue Service (SQS)

SQS is a fully managed message queue service that decouples producers and consumers.

- **Use Case**:

     o Processing customer orders in an e-commerce application.

- **Workflow**:

1.   Orders are added to an SQS queue by an API Gateway-triggered Lambda function.

     2. A separate Lambda function processes messages from the queue and updates inventory in DynamoDB.

- **Example Code**:

     o **Producer**:

python

```
import boto3

sqs = boto3.client('sqs')
queue_url                =                'https://sqs.us-east-
1.amazonaws.com/123456789012/MyQueue'

def lambda_handler(event, context):
    response = sqs.send_message(
        QueueUrl=queue_url,
        MessageBody='{"order_id": "123", "status": "new"}'
    )
    return response
```

     o **Consumer**:

python

```python
import boto3
import json

sqs = boto3.client('sqs')
queue_url = 'https://sqs.us-east-1.amazonaws.com/123456789012/MyQueue'

def lambda_handler(event, context):
    for record in event['Records']:
        message = json.loads(record['body'])
        print(f"Processing order: {message['order_id']}")
```

2. Amazon Simple Notification Service (SNS)

SNS is a fully managed pub/sub messaging service for broadcasting messages to multiple subscribers.

- **Use Case**:
  - o Broadcasting system alerts to multiple teams via email and SMS.
- **Workflow**:
1. Events are published to an SNS topic.
   2. Subscribers (email, SMS, Lambda) receive notifications.
- **Example**:

python

```
import boto3

sns = boto3.client('sns')
topic_arn = 'arn:aws:sns:us-east-1:123456789012:MyTopic'

def lambda_handler(event, context):
    response = sns.publish(
      TopicArn=topic_arn,
      Message='System alert: High CPU usage detected.',
      Subject='System Alert'
    )
    return response
```

---

3. Amazon EventBridge

EventBridge is a serverless event bus that connects applications using event patterns.

- **Use Case**:
  - Building a serverless data pipeline for processing uploaded files.
- **Workflow**:
1. File uploads to S3 trigger events routed through EventBridge.
   2. EventBridge routes events to a Lambda function for processing.
   3. Processed data is stored in DynamoDB.
- **Event Rule Example**:

json

```json
{
    "Source": ["aws.s3"],
    "DetailType": ["Object Created"],
    "Resources": ["arn:aws:s3:::my-bucket"],
    "Detail": {
        "eventName": ["PutObject"]
    }
}
```

Practical Applications of Event-Driven Patterns

Event-driven architectures enable a wide range of real-world applications.

1. Real-Time Analytics

- **Scenario**:
    - o A social media platform analyzes user interactions in real time.
- **Solution**:
    - o Use Kinesis to capture event streams (e.g., likes, comments).
    - o Lambda processes events and updates real-time dashboards.

2. Workflow Automation

- **Scenario**:
    - o Automating document approval workflows.
- **Solution**:
    1. A user uploads a document to S3.
    2. S3 triggers a Lambda function that starts an approval process via Step Functions.
    3. Approvers are notified via SNS, and final decisions are logged in DynamoDB.

3. IoT Data Processing

- **Scenario**:
    - o Processing temperature readings from thousands of IoT devices.
- **Solution**:
    - o IoT Core routes events to Lambda for processing.
    - o EventBridge filters data to trigger alerts for anomalies.

4. Microservices Integration

- **Scenario**:

- o Coordinating multiple microservices in an e-commerce platform.
- **Solution**:
  - o EventBridge orchestrates events between services (e.g., inventory, payment, shipping).
  - o Each service subscribes to relevant events and processes them independently.

---

5. Customer Notifications

- **Scenario**:
  - o Sending personalized offers to customers based on activity.
- **Solution**:
  - o User activity events are sent to EventBridge.
  - o EventBridge routes events to a Lambda function that generates and sends personalized emails.

Best Practices for Event-Driven Architectures

1. **Decouple Components**:
   - o Use event brokers like SQS, SNS, or EventBridge to decouple producers and consumers.
2. **Optimize Event Processing**:

  o Use batch processing for high-throughput systems to reduce costs and improve efficiency.

3. **Ensure Idempotency**:

  o Design consumers to handle duplicate events gracefully.

4. **Monitor and Debug**:

  o Use CloudWatch and X-Ray to monitor event flows and debug errors.

5. **Implement Security**:

  o Use IAM policies to restrict access to event sources and destinations.

Event-driven architectures enhance scalability, flexibility, and resilience in serverless applications. By leveraging AWS services like SQS, SNS, and EventBridge, developers can design powerful systems that respond to real-time events. With practical examples and best practices, this chapter equips you to build robust event-driven solutions.

Chapter 17: Leveraging Lambda Layers

Lambda Layers are a powerful feature of AWS Lambda that enable you to package and share code, libraries, and runtime dependencies across multiple functions. This chapter introduces Lambda Layers, explains how to create and deploy them, and provides real-world use cases to demonstrate their practical benefits.

What are Lambda Layers?

Lambda Layers are a mechanism to share common code and dependencies between multiple Lambda functions without duplicating them in each function package.

---

1. Key Features of Lambda Layers

- **Code Reusability**:
  - o Centralize shared libraries, utilities, or frameworks to avoid duplication across functions.
- **Reduced Deployment Size**:
  - o Keep function packages small by externalizing large dependencies.
- **Layer Versioning**:
  - o Layers support versioning, allowing functions to use specific versions of shared dependencies.

- **Wide Compatibility**:
    - o Compatible with all Lambda runtimes, including Python, Node.js, Java, and Go.

---

2. Structure of a Lambda Layer

A Lambda Layer contains files organized as they would appear in the Lambda runtime environment.

- **Example Structure**:

bash

```
layer/
└── python/        # For Python runtime
    └── my_library/
        ├── utils.py
        └── __init__.py
```

- Common folders by runtime:
    - o **Python**: python/
    - o **Node.js**: nodejs/
    - o **Java**: java/lib/

---

3. Benefits of Using Lambda Layers

- **Simplified Maintenance**:

- Update dependencies in a single place instead of updating every function.
- **Improved Performance**:
  - Reduces cold start times by keeping function packages lightweight.
- **Collaboration**:
  - Share layers across teams or accounts.

Creating and Deploying Shared Libraries

---

1. Preparing a Lambda Layer

- Create the directory structure for your layer:

bash

```
mkdir -p my-layer/python
cd my-layer/python
```

- Add dependencies:
  - For Python:

  bash

  ```
  pip install requests -t .
  ```

o   For Node.js:

bash

```
mkdir -p nodejs
cd nodejs
npm install lodash
```

2. Packaging the Layer

- Zip the contents of the directory:

bash

```
cd ..
zip -r my-layer.zip .
```

3. Deploying the Layer

- Use the AWS CLI to create a new Lambda Layer:

bash

```
aws lambda publish-layer-version \
  --layer-name my-shared-layer \
  --description "Common libraries for my Lambda functions" \
  --license-info "MIT" \
  --compatible-runtimes python3.9 \
  --zip-file fileb://my-layer.zip
```

- Note the LayerVersionArn in the output.

---

4. Adding the Layer to a Lambda Function

- In the AWS Management Console:
    1. Navigate to your Lambda function.
    2. Under **Configuration**, select **Layers** and click **Add a Layer**.
    3. Choose the custom layer and select the appropriate version.
- Using the AWS CLI:

bash

```
aws lambda update-function-configuration \
  --function-name my-function \
  --layers    arn:aws:lambda:us-east-1:123456789012:layer:my-shared-layer:1
```

---

5. Testing the Function

- Access the layer's contents in your function:
    - **Python Example**:

python

```python
import requests

def lambda_handler(event, context):
    response = requests.get("https://api.example.com/data")
    return response.json()
```

Real-World Use Cases for Layers

1. Shared Utilities

- **Scenario**:
  - Multiple Lambda functions need access to custom utilities (e.g., logging or data formatting).
- **Solution**:
  - Package the utilities as a Lambda Layer and share them across functions.
- **Example**:
  - A logging utility:

python

```python
# In the layer (my_layer/python/my_logging.py)
import logging

def setup_logger():
    logger = logging.getLogger()
    logger.setLevel(logging.INFO)
```

```
return logger
```

2. Common Dependencies

- **Scenario**:
    - Many functions rely on the same third-party libraries, such as boto3 or numpy.
- **Solution**:
    - Package these libraries in a shared layer to reduce duplication and deployment size.

3. Machine Learning Models

- **Scenario**:
    - A machine learning application uses pre-trained models for inference.
- **Solution**:
    - Store the models in a Lambda Layer for centralized access by inference functions.
- **Example**:
    - Deploy a TensorFlow model in the /opt directory using a layer.

4. Custom Runtime

- **Scenario**:

  o A function requires a runtime not natively supported by AWS Lambda.

- **Solution**:

  o Create a custom runtime as a Lambda Layer.

- **Example**:

  o Deploy a Ruby runtime as a layer for Lambda functions.

---

5. Security Libraries

- **Scenario**:

  o Functions need to implement consistent security practices, such as JWT validation.

- **Solution**:

  o Package security libraries and configurations in a shared layer.

- **Example**:

  o A library for validating OAuth tokens:

  python

  ```
  # In the layer (my_layer/python/security.py)
  import jwt

  def validate_token(token, secret):
  ```

```
return jwt.decode(token, secret, algorithms=["HS256"])
```

Best Practices for Using Lambda Layers

1. **Keep Layers Lightweight**:
   - Avoid including unnecessary files to minimize layer size.
2. **Version Control**:
   - Use layer versioning to ensure compatibility and avoid breaking changes.
3. **Monitor and Update Dependencies**:
   - Regularly update shared libraries to address vulnerabilities.
4. **Document Layer Contents**:
   - Clearly document what each layer contains to improve team collaboration.
5. **Secure Access**:
   - Use IAM policies to restrict access to sensitive layers.

Lambda Layers streamline the development of serverless applications by promoting code reusability, reducing duplication, and simplifying maintenance. By understanding how to create, deploy, and manage layers, developers can enhance the scalability and efficiency of their serverless architectures.

Chapter 18: Serverless Application Testing

Testing is a crucial aspect of building reliable serverless applications. Serverless testing requires special attention due to the distributed and event-driven nature of serverless architectures. This chapter covers unit testing for Lambda functions, end-to-end testing for serverless workflows, and real-world strategies to ensure robust application performance.

Unit Testing Lambda Functions

Unit testing focuses on testing individual components (functions) in isolation from their dependencies.

---

1. Why Unit Testing is Important

- Ensures function logic behaves as expected.
- Identifies issues early in the development lifecycle.
- Simplifies debugging by isolating failures to specific components.

---

2. Setting Up a Unit Testing Environment

- **Choose a Testing Framework**:
  - o Python: pytest, unittest
  - o Node.js: Jest, Mocha
  - o Java: JUnit
- **Mock Dependencies**:
  - o Mock external services, SDKs, and resources using libraries like moto (Python) or jest-mock-aws (Node.js).

---

3. Writing Unit Tests for Lambda

- **Example**: Python Lambda function that processes an S3 event.

python

```python
import boto3

def lambda_handler(event, context):
    s3 = boto3.client('s3')
    bucket = event['Records'][0]['s3']['bucket']['name']
    key = event['Records'][0]['s3']['object']['key']

    # Process the S3 object
    response = s3.get_object(Bucket=bucket, Key=key)
    return            {"status":            "success",            "content":
response['Body'].read().decode('utf-8')}
```

- **Unit Test with Mocks**:

python

```python
import pytest
from unittest.mock import patch
from lambda_function import lambda_handler


@patch('lambda_function.boto3.client')
def test_lambda_handler(mock_boto3):
    # Mock S3 response
    mock_s3 = mock_boto3.return_value
    mock_s3.get_object.return_value = {
        'Body': b'Mock file content'
    }

    # Mock event
    event = {
        "Records": [
            {
                "s3": {
                    "bucket": {"name": "test-bucket"},
                    "object": {"key": "test-key"}
                }
            }
        ]
    }

    # Invoke function
    response = lambda_handler(event, None)
    assert response['status'] == 'success'
    assert response['content'] == 'Mock file content'
```

4. Best Practices for Unit Testing

- Mock external services and resources.
- Write tests for edge cases and error scenarios.
- Ensure functions are idempotent to handle retries gracefully.

End-to-End Testing for Serverless Workflows

End-to-end (E2E) testing validates the entire application workflow, ensuring all components work together as expected.

1. Why E2E Testing is Important

- Validates interactions between services and components.
- Ensures real-world scenarios are handled correctly.
- Identifies integration issues in distributed systems.

2. Setting Up an E2E Testing Environment

- Use a staging environment that mirrors production.
- Enable logging and monitoring (CloudWatch, X-Ray) for detailed insights.
- Isolate test data to avoid conflicts with production data.

3. Example E2E Workflow Testing

- **Scenario**: Processing files uploaded to S3.
  1. A file is uploaded to S3.
  2. S3 triggers a Lambda function to process the file.
  3. The processed result is stored in DynamoDB.
- **Testing Steps**:
  - Upload a test file to the S3 bucket.
  - Verify that the Lambda function is triggered and processes the file correctly.
  - Check that the processed data is saved in DynamoDB.
- **Automating E2E Tests**:
  - Use AWS SDKs or frameworks like pytest (Python) or Cypress (JavaScript) for automation.
  - **Example Python E2E Test**:

    python

    ```python
    import boto3

    def test_end_to_end_workflow():
        # S3 client
        s3 = boto3.client('s3')
        bucket_name = 'test-bucket'
        key = 'test-file.txt'

        # Upload test file
    ```

```
s3.put_object(Bucket=bucket_name,          Key=key,
Body='Sample content')

# Verify DynamoDB entry
dynamodb = boto3.resource('dynamodb')
table = dynamodb.Table('ProcessedFiles')
response = table.get_item(Key={'file_key': key})
assert 'Item' in response
```

4. Tools for E2E Testing

- **Local Testing**:
  - AWS SAM CLI or LocalStack to simulate AWS services locally.
- **Cloud Testing**:
  - Execute tests in a staging environment to replicate production conditions.

Real-World Testing Strategies

Combining unit, integration, and E2E testing ensures comprehensive test coverage.

1. Automate Testing Pipelines

- Use CI/CD tools like AWS CodePipeline, Jenkins, or GitHub Actions to automate testing workflows.
- Trigger tests automatically on code commits or deployments.

2. Test for Failure Scenarios

- Simulate failures to ensure the application handles errors gracefully.
- Examples:
  - Throttling in SQS.
  - Network failures during API calls.

3. Validate Performance

- Use load testing tools (e.g., Artillery, Apache JMeter) to evaluate the system under high traffic.
- Monitor latency, error rates, and resource usage.

4. Secure Testing

- Validate security configurations:
  - IAM roles and policies.
  - API Gateway authentication and authorizers.
- Ensure sensitive data is encrypted in transit and at rest.

5. Debugging Tools

- **CloudWatch Logs**:
    - o Analyze logs to identify errors or bottlenecks.
- **AWS X-Ray**:
    - o Trace requests to pinpoint latency issues and debug distributed workflows.

6. Testing Best Practices

- **Test Early and Often**:
    - o Incorporate testing into the development lifecycle.
- **Use Mock Data**:
    - o Avoid testing with production data to prevent conflicts.
- **Isolate Tests**:
    - o Use unique identifiers for test data to avoid overlaps.

Testing serverless applications is essential to ensure reliability, scalability, and resilience. By combining unit testing, E2E testing, and robust testing strategies, developers can build serverless applications that meet high standards of performance and reliability.

Chapter 19: Cost Optimization for Serverless Applications

Serverless architectures inherently provide cost-efficiency, as you pay only for the resources you use. However, optimizing costs further can maximize savings while maintaining performance. This chapter explores AWS Lambda pricing, strategies for reducing costs, and real-world examples of cost-saving techniques.

Understanding AWS Lambda Pricing

AWS Lambda pricing is based on two main components: **invocations** and **execution duration**.

---

1. Invocations

- **Definition**: The number of times a Lambda function is invoked.
- **Pricing**:
  - First **1 million invocations** per month are free.
  - After that, $0.20 per 1 million invocations.
- **Examples**:
  - 2 million invocations/month:
    - 1 million free

- 1 million charged = $0.20

---

2. Execution Duration

- **Definition**: The time a function runs, rounded up to the nearest millisecond.
- **Pricing**:
  - Charged based on the allocated memory and execution time.
  - **Formula**:

    text

    Cost = (Memory (GB) × Duration (ms) × Requests) × Price

  - **Example**:
    - Memory: 128 MB (0.125 GB)
    - Duration: 200 ms
    - Invocations: 1 million
    - Price: $0.00001667/GB-s
    - **Total Cost**:

      bash

      (0.125 × 0.2 × 1,000,000) × $0.00001667 = $0.42

---

3. Additional Costs

- **Provisioned Concurrency**:
  - Charged for pre-warmed instances.
  - Pricing depends on memory and duration.
- **Data Transfer**:
  - Outbound data transfer is charged separately.
- **Associated Services**:
  - Costs from services like API Gateway, S3, or DynamoDB.

Strategies for Reducing Costs

Cost optimization involves minimizing resource usage, eliminating unnecessary invocations, and choosing cost-effective solutions.

---

1. Optimize Function Execution

- **Streamline Code**:
  - Remove unnecessary operations and external calls.
  - Example:
    - Cache API responses locally within the function to reduce repeated calls.
- **Optimize Logic**:
  - Use efficient algorithms and batch processing.

- o Example:
  - Process multiple SQS messages in a single batch rather than individually.

2. Right-Size Memory Allocation

- **Tuning Memory**:
  - o Adjust memory allocation to find the balance between cost and performance.
  - o Higher memory reduces execution time but increases cost per millisecond.
- **Tools**:
  - o Use AWS Lambda Power Tuning tools to determine the optimal memory configuration.

3. Use Provisioned Concurrency Wisely

- **When to Use**:
  - o For latency-sensitive applications with predictable traffic spikes.
- **Optimization**:
  - o Enable provisioned concurrency only during high-traffic periods.

4. Avoid Unnecessary Invocations

- **Event Filtering**:
  - Filter events at the source to prevent invoking Lambda unnecessarily.
  - Example:
    - Use S3 event filters to trigger Lambda only for .jpg uploads.
- **Debounce Triggers**:
  - Prevent duplicate invocations by combining multiple triggers into a single event.

---

5. Leverage Free Tiers

- **Free Tier Usage**:
  - Take advantage of the 1 million free requests and 400,000 GB-seconds per month.
- **Combine Free Services**:
  - Use DynamoDB free tier for small workloads.

---

6. Use Reserved Concurrency

- **Purpose**:
  - Limit the number of concurrent executions to control costs.

- **Example**:
  - o Set reserved concurrency to 10 for non-critical functions to prevent unexpected spikes.

---

7. Monitor and Optimize Usage

- **CloudWatch Metrics**:
  - o Monitor invocation counts, duration, and memory usage.
- **Billing Alarms**:
  - o Set alarms in the AWS Billing Dashboard to track costs.

---

8. Optimize Associated Services

- **API Gateway**:
  - o Use **HTTP APIs** instead of REST APIs for cost savings in simple use cases.
- **S3**:
  - o Use S3 Intelligent-Tiering for storage to optimize costs.
- **DynamoDB**:
  - o Use on-demand or provisioned capacity based on usage patterns.

Real-World Cost-Saving Examples

1. E-Commerce Application

- **Scenario**:
  - o A platform handles millions of product searches and orders daily.
- **Challenges**:
  - o High invocation costs due to inefficient API Gateway usage.
- **Solution**:
  - o Switched from REST APIs to HTTP APIs, reducing API Gateway costs by 70%.
  - o Tuned Lambda memory to minimize execution time.
- **Results**:
  - o Saved $2,000 per month on infrastructure costs.

2. Media Processing Pipeline

- **Scenario**:
  - o A media company processes thousands of videos uploaded daily.
- **Challenges**:

- High costs from redundant Lambda invocations and large payloads.

- **Solution**:
  - Introduced event filtering for S3 to process only .mp4 files.
  - Batched video metadata updates to DynamoDB.

- **Results**:
  - Reduced invocation costs by 40%.

---

3. Real-Time Analytics

- **Scenario**:
  - A real-time analytics platform processes IoT data from thousands of devices.

- **Challenges**:
  - High data processing costs due to over-provisioning of resources.

- **Solution**:
  - Tuned memory allocation using AWS Lambda Power Tuning.
  - Aggregated events in Kinesis before processing with Lambda.

- **Results**:
  - Reduced Lambda execution costs by 50%.

4. Customer Notification System

- **Scenario**:
  - A notification service sends alerts via SNS triggered by EventBridge.
- **Challenges**:
  - Excessive invocations due to duplicate events.
- **Solution**:
  - Implemented deduplication logic in the event source.
  - Batched notifications to reduce SNS publishing costs.
- **Results**:
  - Saved $500 monthly in SNS and Lambda costs.

Best Practices for Cost Optimization

1. **Test in a Staging Environment**:
   - Monitor costs in a non-production setup before scaling.
2. **Consolidate Functions**:
   - Combine related tasks into fewer Lambda functions to reduce invocation overhead.
3. **Use Savings Plans**:
   - Purchase AWS Savings Plans for consistent workloads to save on Lambda costs.

4. **Monitor Regularly**:

   o Continuously analyze CloudWatch and billing data for optimization opportunities.

5. **Design for Scalability**:

   o Build architectures that scale efficiently under load.

AWS Lambda's pricing model ensures cost efficiency, but careful design and optimization can lead to even greater savings. By understanding Lambda pricing, applying optimization strategies, and leveraging AWS monitoring tools, you can build scalable and cost-effective serverless applications.

Chapter 20: Serverless Machine Learning with Lambda

AWS Lambda provides an efficient and scalable platform for deploying machine learning (ML) models. By combining Lambda with AWS ML services like SageMaker, you can create robust, serverless ML pipelines. This chapter explores deploying ML models on Lambda, integrating SageMaker with Lambda, and showcases real-world examples of serverless ML deployments.

Introduction to Deploying ML Models on Lambda

AWS Lambda's serverless nature makes it an excellent choice for ML model inference workloads, particularly when you need scalability and cost-efficiency.

---

1. Why Use Lambda for ML Models?

- **Scalability**: Automatically scales to handle varying inference requests.
- **Cost-Effectiveness**: Pay only for the compute time and memory used.
- **Ease of Integration**: Seamlessly connects with other AWS services like S3, API Gateway, and DynamoDB.

2. Considerations for Deploying ML Models on Lambda

- **Model Size**:
    - o Lambda has a deployment package size limit of 250 MB (including layers).
    - o Optimize model size using techniques like quantization or pruning.
- **Execution Time**:
    - o Lambda has a maximum execution time of 15 minutes. Ensure inference tasks can complete within this limit.
- **Memory Allocation**:
    - o Allocate sufficient memory for inference tasks. More memory also means higher CPU allocation, reducing latency.

3. Common ML Use Cases for Lambda

- **Real-Time Predictions**:
    - o E.g., fraud detection, recommendation systems.
- **Data Processing**:
    - o Preprocessing data for downstream ML pipelines.
- **Lightweight Models**:

o   Running models like logistic regression or small neural networks.

Using AWS Services Like SageMaker and Lambda Together

AWS SageMaker is a fully managed ML service that complements Lambda for both training and serving models.

---

1. Leveraging SageMaker for Model Training

- **Training Overview**:
    o   SageMaker trains ML models using large datasets and scalable compute resources.
    o   Models are stored in S3 upon completion.
- **Workflow**:
1.   Train a model in SageMaker.
    2. Export the model artifact to an S3 bucket.
    3. Deploy the model using SageMaker Endpoints or Lambda for inference.

---

2. Invoking SageMaker Endpoints from Lambda

- **Why Use SageMaker Endpoints?**

- o SageMaker endpoints provide persistent hosting for ML models, optimized for low-latency predictions.
- o Lambda can invoke these endpoints for real-time inference.

- **Example Workflow**:

1. Lambda receives an event (e.g., API Gateway request).
    2. Lambda forwards the input to a SageMaker endpoint.
    3. The endpoint returns the prediction.

- **Example Code**:

```python
python

import boto3

runtime = boto3.client('runtime.sagemaker')

def lambda_handler(event, context):
    endpoint_name = 'my-sagemaker-endpoint'
    payload = event['body']

    response = runtime.invoke_endpoint(
        EndpointName=endpoint_name,
        ContentType='application/json',
        Body=payload
    )

    result = response['Body'].read().decode('utf-8')
    return {
        'statusCode': 200,
```

```
    'body': result

  }
```

---

3. Deploying Models Directly on Lambda

For lightweight models, you can package the model with the Lambda function.

- **Example Workflow**:
    1. Preprocess the data in Lambda.
    2. Load the model during the function initialization phase.
    3. Perform inference and return results.
- **Example Code (Python with Scikit-Learn)**:

```python
python

import joblib
import json

# Load the model during initialization
model = joblib.load('/opt/model/model.pkl')

def lambda_handler(event, context):
    data = json.loads(event['body'])
    prediction = model.predict([data['features']])
    return {
        'statusCode': 200,
```

```
'body': json.dumps({'prediction': prediction.tolist()})
}
```

- **Best Practices**:
  - ○ Use Lambda layers to package model dependencies and reduce deployment size.
  - ○ Minimize cold start times by optimizing model loading.

Real-World ML Deployment Examples

---

1. Real-Time Fraud Detection

- **Scenario**:
  - ○ A payment gateway processes transactions and detects fraud in real time.
- **Workflow**:
  1. Transactions are sent to Lambda via API Gateway.
  2. Lambda forwards the data to a SageMaker endpoint hosting an anomaly detection model.
  3. The endpoint returns a fraud score, and Lambda decides whether to allow or block the transaction.
- **Benefits**:
  - ○ Low-latency decision-making.

o   Scalable and cost-efficient architecture.

---

2. Image Classification Pipeline

- **Scenario**:
  - o   A photo-sharing platform classifies uploaded images for tagging.
- **Workflow**:
  1. S3 triggers Lambda when an image is uploaded.
  2. Lambda uses a pre-trained TensorFlow Lite model to classify the image.
  3. Results are stored in DynamoDB.
- **Benefits**:
  - o   Fully serverless pipeline.
  - o   Minimal operational overhead.

---

3. Sentiment Analysis API

- **Scenario**:
  - o   A SaaS platform analyzes customer feedback for sentiment.
- **Workflow**:
  1. Customer feedback is sent to Lambda via API Gateway.

2. Lambda performs preprocessing and sends the data to a SageMaker endpoint hosting a sentiment analysis model.

3. The result is returned to the client.

- **Benefits**:
  - o Easy integration with web applications.
  - o Handles varying workloads seamlessly.

4. Predictive Maintenance for IoT Devices

- **Scenario**:
  - o IoT sensors collect device performance metrics and predict failures.
- **Workflow**:
  1. IoT Core streams data to Lambda.
  2. Lambda preprocesses the data and calls a SageMaker endpoint for prediction.
  3. Alerts are sent via SNS for devices likely to fail.
- **Benefits**:
  - o Proactive maintenance reduces downtime.
  - o Efficient processing of real-time data streams.

5. Personalized Recommendations

- **Scenario**:
  - ○ An e-commerce site provides personalized product recommendations.
- **Workflow**:
  1. User actions (e.g., browsing or purchases) generate events routed to Lambda.
  2. Lambda queries a SageMaker endpoint hosting a recommendation model.
  3. Recommendations are returned to the user in real time.
- **Benefits**:
  - ○ Enhanced user experience.
  - ○ Scalable to handle high traffic.

Best Practices for Serverless ML

1. **Optimize Model Size**:
   - ○ Use model compression techniques like quantization or pruning for smaller deployment packages.
2. **Monitor and Update Models**:
   - ○ Regularly retrain and update models using SageMaker to maintain accuracy.
3. **Optimize Lambda Configuration**:
   - ○ Allocate sufficient memory for fast inference.

o   Use provisioned concurrency for latency-sensitive applications.

4. **Use Layers for Dependencies**:

o   Package large libraries (e.g., TensorFlow, PyTorch) as Lambda layers to reduce function size.

5. **Leverage SageMaker for Large Models**:

o   For complex or large models, use SageMaker endpoints instead of deploying directly on Lambda.

Serverless machine learning with AWS Lambda enables scalable and cost-effective deployment of ML models. Whether integrating with SageMaker for powerful inference or deploying lightweight models directly, Lambda provides flexibility for a wide range of ML applications. By understanding best practices and leveraging AWS services, you can build robust serverless ML solutions.

Chapter 21: Building Real-Time Applications

Real-time applications enable instantaneous communication and live updates, providing dynamic user experiences. AWS Lambda and API Gateway are well-suited for building serverless real-time applications. This chapter covers implementing WebSocket APIs, building real-time dashboards and chat apps, and provides a hands-on example to demonstrate these concepts.

Implementing WebSocket APIs with Lambda and API Gateway
WebSocket APIs allow for full-duplex communication between clients and servers, enabling real-time data exchange.

---

1. Overview of WebSocket APIs

- **What Are WebSockets?**
  - WebSockets establish a persistent connection, allowing bidirectional communication between clients and servers.
  - Ideal for real-time applications like chat apps, live dashboards, and gaming platforms.
- **API Gateway and WebSockets:**

o Amazon API Gateway manages WebSocket connections and routes messages to AWS Lambda functions.

2. Key Components of WebSocket APIs

- **Routes**:
  - o **$connect**: Triggered when a client connects to the WebSocket API.
  - o **$disconnect**: Triggered when a client disconnects.
  - o **Custom Routes**: Handle specific client messages (e.g., sendMessage).
- **Connection ID**:
  - o A unique identifier for each client connection, used for sending messages.
- **Integration with Lambda**:
  - o Lambda functions process WebSocket events and execute custom logic.

3. Setting Up a WebSocket API

- **Step 1: Create a WebSocket API in API Gateway**
  1. Open the API Gateway Console.
  2. Choose **Create API** > **WebSocket API**.

3. Define a WebSocket route (e.g., $connect, $disconnect, sendMessage).

- **Step 2: Create Lambda Functions**
  - Create separate functions for $connect, $disconnect, and custom routes.
  - Example ($connect):

  python

  ```python
  def lambda_handler(event, context):
      connection_id = event['requestContext']['connectionId']
      print(f"Connection established: {connection_id}")
      return {"statusCode": 200}
  ```

- **Step 3: Deploy the API**
  - Deploy the WebSocket API to a stage (e.g., dev).
  - Note the WebSocket URL (e.g., wss://api-id.execute-api.region.amazonaws.com/dev).

- **Step 4: Manage Connections**
  - Use the connectionId to send messages to clients.
  - Example (Python):

  python

  ```python
  import boto3
  ```

```
apigateway      =       boto3.client('apigatewaymanagementapi',
endpoint_url="https://api-id.execute-
api.region.amazonaws.com/dev")


def send_message(connection_id, message):


apigateway.post_to_connection(ConnectionId=connection_id,
Data=message)
```

Building Real-Time Dashboards and Chat Apps

Real-time dashboards and chat applications are common use cases for WebSocket APIs.

1. Real-Time Dashboards

- **Use Case**:
    - o A live dashboard displays metrics like stock prices, server health, or user activity.
- **Architecture**:

1.   Data sources (e.g., IoT devices, APIs) send updates to an EventBridge or SQS queue.

2. Lambda functions process the updates and send messages to connected WebSocket clients.

- **Benefits**:
    - o Instant updates to multiple users.

o Serverless architecture eliminates the need for dedicated WebSocket servers.

---

2. Real-Time Chat Applications

- **Use Case**:
  - o A chat app allows users to exchange messages in real time.
- **Architecture**:
1. Clients connect to the WebSocket API and establish sessions.
   2. Messages are routed to Lambda functions, which relay them to other connected clients.
   3. DynamoDB stores session and chat data for persistence.
- **Features**:
  - o Group chats.
  - o Message persistence.
  - o Notifications for new messages.

Hands-On Real-Time Application Example

Scenario: A real-time chat application using Lambda and WebSocket API.

---

1. Architecture Overview

- **API Gateway**:
  - Manages WebSocket connections and routes messages.
- **Lambda Functions**:
  - **$connect**: Handles new client connections.
  - **$disconnect**: Cleans up resources when clients disconnect.
  - **sendMessage**: Processes and broadcasts messages.
- **DynamoDB**:
  - Stores client connection details.

---

2. Implementation

- **Step 1: Define WebSocket Routes**
  - $connect
  - $disconnect
  - sendMessage

Step 2: Create Lambda Functions

- **$connect Function**:

python

```python
import boto3

dynamodb = boto3.resource('dynamodb')
table = dynamodb.Table('ConnectionsTable')

def lambda_handler(event, context):
    connection_id = event['requestContext']['connectionId']
    table.put_item(Item={'connectionId': connection_id})
    print(f"Connection added: {connection_id}")
    return {"statusCode": 200}
```

- **$disconnect Function**:

python

```python
def lambda_handler(event, context):
    connection_id = event['requestContext']['connectionId']
    table.delete_item(Key={'connectionId': connection_id})
    print(f"Connection removed: {connection_id}")
    return {"statusCode": 200}
```

- **sendMessage Function**:

python

```python
def lambda_handler(event, context):
    connection_id = event['requestContext']['connectionId']
    message = event['body']

    # Fetch all connections
    connections = table.scan()['Items']
```

```python
for conn in connections:
    try:

        apigateway.post_to_connection(ConnectionId=conn['connectionId'],
        Data=message)
    except Exception as e:
        print(f"Error sending message: {e}")

    return {"statusCode": 200}
```

Step 3: Deploy the Application

- Deploy the WebSocket API and Lambda functions.
- Create a DynamoDB table (ConnectionsTable) to store connection IDs.

Step 4: Test the Application

1. Connect a WebSocket client to the API Gateway URL.
2. Send a message:
   o Example:

   json

   ```json
   {
   "action": "sendMessage",
   "data": "Hello, world!"
   ```

}

3. Verify that all connected clients receive the message.

Best Practices for Real-Time Applications

1. **Optimize for Scalability**:
   - o Use DynamoDB Streams or SQS to handle high traffic.
2. **Secure Connections**:
   - o Implement authentication for WebSocket connections (e.g., JWT tokens).
3. **Monitor Usage**:
   - o Use CloudWatch metrics to monitor WebSocket connections and message throughput.
4. **Error Handling**:
   - o Handle dropped connections gracefully and clean up resources.

Building real-time applications with AWS Lambda and API Gateway enables scalable, cost-efficient, and highly responsive solutions. By leveraging WebSocket APIs, developers can implement live dashboards, chat apps, and other real-time systems with ease. The hands-on example provided in this chapter serves as a practical foundation for developing serverless real-time applications.

Chapter 22: Serverless IoT Applications

AWS IoT Core, combined with AWS Lambda, provides a powerful and scalable platform for building IoT applications. This chapter explores integrating AWS IoT Core with Lambda, discusses real-world IoT use cases, and provides a hands-on example of building a simple IoT pipeline.

Integrating AWS IoT Core with Lambda

AWS IoT Core is a managed service that connects IoT devices to the cloud. By integrating IoT Core with Lambda, you can process device messages, trigger workflows, and analyze IoT data.

---

1. Key Features of AWS IoT Core

- **Device Communication**:
    - Supports MQTT, HTTPS, and WebSocket protocols for secure communication with devices.
- **Rules Engine**:
    - Routes incoming messages from devices to AWS services like Lambda, DynamoDB, or S3.
- **Device Shadow**:
    - Maintains a virtual representation of device state for offline and remote management.

2. Steps to Integrate AWS IoT Core with Lambda

- **Step 1: Set Up IoT Core**
  - Create an IoT thing for your device.
  - Register the device and download its security certificates.

- **Step 2: Create an IoT Rule**
  - Define a rule to route messages to Lambda.
  - Example SQL statement for filtering messages:

  sql

  ```
  SELECT * FROM 'iot/topic/sensor'
  ```

- **Step 3: Create a Lambda Function**
  - Lambda processes messages from IoT devices.
  - Example:

  python

  ```python
  import json

  def lambda_handler(event, context):
      print(f"Received IoT message: {json.dumps(event)}")
      return {"statusCode": 200, "body": "Message processed"}
  ```

- **Step 4: Link IoT Rule to Lambda**

- o   Configure the rule to invoke the Lambda function whenever a message is received.
- **Step 5: Test the Setup**
  - o   Publish messages to the MQTT topic (iot/topic/sensor) and verify that Lambda processes them.

Real-World Examples of IoT Use Cases

IoT applications span a wide range of industries, including manufacturing, healthcare, and transportation.

---

1. Smart Home Automation

- **Scenario**:
  - o   Smart home devices, such as thermostats and lights, are controlled remotely.
- **Solution**:
  - o   Devices send state updates to IoT Core.
  - o   Lambda processes commands from users to control devices.
- **Example**:
  - o   Voice commands to a smart speaker trigger Lambda to adjust thermostat settings.

---

2. Predictive Maintenance

- **Scenario**:
  - Industrial machinery sends performance metrics to the cloud for analysis.
- **Solution**:
  - IoT Core collects telemetry data from machines.
  - Lambda processes the data and invokes SageMaker for anomaly detection.
- **Example**:
  - A manufacturing plant predicts equipment failures before they occur, reducing downtime.

---

3. Fleet Management

- **Scenario**:
  - A logistics company tracks vehicle locations and performance in real time.
- **Solution**:
  - Vehicles send GPS and diagnostic data to IoT Core.
  - Lambda stores the data in DynamoDB for real-time tracking.
- **Example**:
  - A dashboard shows live locations and fuel levels of all fleet vehicles.

4. Healthcare Monitoring

- **Scenario**:
    - o Wearable devices monitor patient vitals and alert doctors to anomalies.
- **Solution**:
    - o IoT Core routes health data to Lambda for processing.
    - o Alerts are sent to doctors via SNS for critical conditions.
- **Example**:
    - o A smartwatch detects an irregular heartbeat and notifies a healthcare provider.

5. Environmental Monitoring

- **Scenario**:
    - o Sensors monitor air quality, temperature, and humidity for research.
- **Solution**:
    - o IoT Core aggregates sensor data and triggers Lambda for analysis.
    - o Results are stored in S3 for further study.
- **Example**:
    - o Real-time air quality monitoring in urban areas.

Building a Simple IoT Pipeline

Scenario: Build a serverless pipeline to monitor and process temperature readings from IoT devices.

1. Architecture Overview

- **IoT Device**:
  - Sends temperature readings to an MQTT topic.
- **AWS IoT Core**:
  - Routes messages to a Lambda function.
- **AWS Lambda**:
  - Processes the data and stores it in DynamoDB.
- **DynamoDB**:
  - Stores processed data for further analysis.

2. Implementation Steps

- **Step 1: Configure IoT Core**
  1. Create an IoT thing and download its security certificates.
  2. Create an MQTT topic (iot/topic/temperature) for device messages.
- **Step 2: Create an IoT Rule**

- o SQL statement to filter temperature readings:

sql

SELECT * FROM 'iot/topic/temperature'

- **Step 3: Create a Lambda Function**
  - o Lambda processes incoming messages and saves them to DynamoDB.
  - o Example Code:

python

```python
import json
import boto3

dynamodb = boto3.resource('dynamodb')
table = dynamodb.Table('TemperatureReadings')

def lambda_handler(event, context):
    for record in event['Records']:
        data = json.loads(record['body'])
        table.put_item(Item={
            'deviceId': data['deviceId'],
            'timestamp': data['timestamp'],
            'temperature': data['temperature']
        })
    return {"statusCode": 200, "body": "Data processed"}
```

- **Step 4: Create a DynamoDB Table**

- o Table name: TemperatureReadings.
- o Partition key: deviceId.
- o Sort key: timestamp.

- **Step 5: Test the Pipeline**
  - o Publish a test message to the MQTT topic:

json

```json
{
  "deviceId": "device123",
  "timestamp": "2025-01-15T10:00:00Z",
  "temperature": 22.5
}
```

  - o Verify that the data is stored in DynamoDB.

3. Enhancements

- Add CloudWatch metrics to monitor device activity and Lambda performance.
- Integrate SNS to send alerts if temperature readings exceed a threshold.

Best Practices for IoT Applications

1. **Optimize Data Transmission**:
   o Use efficient protocols like MQTT for low-latency communication.

2. **Implement Security**:
   o Use mutual TLS for secure device connections.
   o Regularly rotate device certificates.

3. **Scale Efficiently**:
   o Use DynamoDB Streams or Kinesis for high-velocity data processing.

4. **Monitor and Debug**:
   o Use CloudWatch and AWS IoT Analytics to monitor device activity and troubleshoot issues.

5. **Minimize Latency**:
   o Use AWS Greengrass for local data processing when low latency is critical.

Integrating AWS IoT Core with Lambda unlocks the potential for building scalable and cost-effective IoT applications. Whether it's smart home devices, predictive maintenance, or environmental monitoring, serverless IoT pipelines enable real-time data processing and actionable insights. By following the steps and best practices outlined in this chapter, you can build robust IoT solutions tailored to your specific use case.

Chapter 23: CI/CD for Serverless Applications

Continuous Integration and Continuous Deployment (CI/CD) are essential for maintaining fast, reliable, and automated deployment processes for serverless applications. This chapter covers setting up pipelines with AWS CodePipeline and CodeBuild, automating deployments with GitHub Actions, and showcases real-world CI/CD workflows for Lambda.

Setting Up Pipelines with AWS CodePipeline and CodeBuild

AWS CodePipeline and CodeBuild provide a fully managed solution for automating serverless application builds, tests, and deployments.

---

1. Overview of AWS CI/CD Tools

- **AWS CodePipeline**:
  - Automates the end-to-end release process.
  - Integrates with AWS services and third-party tools.
- **AWS CodeBuild**:
  - Compiles source code, runs tests, and produces build artifacts.

o   Pay-as-you-go pricing ensures cost efficiency.

---

2. Steps to Set Up a Pipeline

- **Step 1: Create a CodePipeline**
  - Open the **CodePipeline Console**.
  - Create a new pipeline and configure the source stage (e.g., GitHub, CodeCommit, or S3).
- **Step 2: Integrate CodeBuild**
  - Create a build project in **AWS CodeBuild**.
  - Define the build specifications in a buildspec.yml file:

yaml

```yaml
version: 0.2

phases:
  install:
    runtime-versions:
      nodejs: 16
    commands:
      - npm install -g aws-cdk
  build:
    commands:
      - npm install
      - npm run build
  post_build:
    commands:
```

```
- aws cloudformation deploy --template-file template.yml -
-stack-name MyServerlessApp
artifacts:
  files:
    - '**/*'
```

- **Step 3: Configure Deployment Stage**
  - Use AWS CloudFormation or AWS SAM to deploy your application.
  - Example SAM command:

```bash
bash
```

```
sam    deploy    --template-file    template.yml    --stack-name
MyServerlessApp --capabilities CAPABILITY_IAM
```

- **Step 4: Test the Pipeline**
  - Commit changes to your source repository and verify that the pipeline triggers build and deployment stages automatically.

---

3. Benefits of CodePipeline and CodeBuild

- **Integration**:
  - Seamlessly integrates with AWS services like Lambda, S3, and DynamoDB.
- **Scalability**:

o   Automatically scales to handle multiple builds simultaneously.

- **Monitoring**:
  - o   Provides detailed execution history and logs for debugging.

Automating Deployments with GitHub Actions

GitHub Actions is a flexible CI/CD tool that integrates directly with GitHub repositories.

---

1. Key Features of GitHub Actions

- **Custom Workflows**:
  - o   Define CI/CD pipelines using YAML files.
- **Marketplace Integrations**:
  - o   Use prebuilt actions for AWS services and serverless frameworks.
- **Event-Driven**:
  - o   Trigger workflows on events like commits, pull requests, or releases.

---

2. Example GitHub Actions Workflow for Lambda

- **Workflow File**: .github/workflows/deploy.yml

yaml

```yaml
name: Deploy to AWS Lambda

on:
  push:
    branches:
      - main

jobs:
  deploy:
    runs-on: ubuntu-latest

    steps:
      - name: Checkout code
        uses: actions/checkout@v3

      - name: Set up Node.js
        uses: actions/setup-node@v3
        with:
          node-version: '16'

      - name: Install dependencies
        run: |
          npm install
          npm install -g aws-cdk

      - name: Build project
```

```
        run: npm run build

      - name: Deploy to AWS
        env:
          AWS_ACCESS_KEY_ID:                        ${{
      secrets.AWS_ACCESS_KEY_ID }}
          AWS_SECRET_ACCESS_KEY:                    ${{
      secrets.AWS_SECRET_ACCESS_KEY }}
          AWS_REGION: us-east-1
        run: cdk deploy --require-approval never
```

3. Secrets Management

- Use GitHub Secrets to store sensitive information like AWS credentials.
  - o Navigate to **Settings** > **Secrets and Variables** > **Actions** > **New Repository Secret**.

4. Testing GitHub Actions

- Push changes to the repository and monitor workflow execution under the **Actions** tab.

Real-World CI/CD Workflows for Lambda

1. Serverless Application Deployment

- **Scenario**:
  - ○ Deploy a Lambda function triggered by API Gateway.
- **Workflow**:
  1. CodePipeline fetches source code from GitHub.
  2. CodeBuild runs tests and packages the Lambda function using AWS SAM.
  3. CodePipeline deploys the function using CloudFormation.

---

2. Multi-Environment Deployment

- **Scenario**:
  - ○ A serverless application requires separate environments for development, staging, and production.
- **Workflow**:
  1. Create separate branches for each environment (e.g., dev, staging, main).
  2. GitHub Actions deploys changes to the corresponding AWS environment.
  3. Example branching strategy:
     - dev → Deploys to MyApp-Dev.

- staging $\to$ Deploys to MyApp-Staging.
- main $\to$ Deploys to MyApp-Production.

---

3. Canary Deployment for Lambda

- **Scenario**:
  - Gradually release a new version of a Lambda function to ensure stability.
- **Workflow**:
  1. CodePipeline creates a new version of the Lambda function.
  2. CodePipeline updates the function's alias to route a small percentage of traffic to the new version.
  3. Monitor logs and metrics in CloudWatch before full deployment.

---

4. Monitoring CI/CD Workflows

- Use CloudWatch Logs for detailed insights into CodeBuild execution.
- Enable SNS notifications in CodePipeline to alert teams of build failures or successful deployments.

Best Practices for Serverless CI/CD

1. **Automate Testing**:
   - Include unit tests, integration tests, and end-to-end tests in the pipeline.

2. **Use Infrastructure as Code**:
   - Define serverless applications using AWS SAM or the Serverless Framework.

3. **Secure Credentials**:
   - Use AWS Secrets Manager or GitHub Secrets for sensitive information.

4. **Enable Rollback**:
   - Configure CloudFormation or SAM deployments to automatically rollback failed changes.

5. **Monitor and Optimize Pipelines**:
   - Use CloudWatch and CodePipeline metrics to monitor performance and identify bottlenecks.

CI/CD pipelines are crucial for ensuring fast and reliable serverless application deployments. AWS CodePipeline, CodeBuild, and GitHub Actions provide flexible and scalable tools to automate the development lifecycle. By following the examples and best practices outlined in this chapter, you can streamline your serverless workflows and enhance productivity.

Chapter 24: Migrating Legacy Applications to Serverless

Migrating legacy applications to a serverless architecture can modernize systems, reduce operational costs, and improve scalability. This chapter explores how to evaluate the feasibility of serverless migration, strategies for breaking down monolithic applications, and provides real-world examples of successful migrations.

Evaluating Serverless Migration Feasibility

Before migrating a legacy application, it's important to assess its suitability for serverless architecture.

---

1. Factors to Consider

- **Application Architecture**:
    - Evaluate if the application can be broken into smaller, independent services.
    - Serverless is ideal for stateless, modular applications.
- **Workload Characteristics**:
    - Serverless excels for applications with:
        - Unpredictable traffic patterns.

- Event-driven workflows.
- Batch processing or real-time analytics.

- **Integration with External Services**:
  o Identify dependencies like databases, APIs, and third-party integrations.
  o Ensure these are compatible with serverless architecture.

- **Compliance and Security**:
  o Assess data privacy, compliance requirements, and security concerns.

- **Performance Requirements**:
  o Evaluate latency tolerance and scalability needs.

2. Tools for Assessment

- **AWS Migration Hub**:
  o Provides insights into application portfolios to assess migration readiness.

- **AWS Well-Architected Tool**:
  o Identifies potential gaps in architecture and readiness for serverless.

Strategies for Breaking Down Monoliths

Monolithic applications often need to be re-architected into smaller, manageable components for a successful serverless migration.

1. Understanding Monolithic Architecture

- **Characteristics**:
  - Single codebase handling all functionalities.
  - Tightly coupled components.
  - Challenges in scaling and deploying specific features.

2. Strangler Fig Pattern

- **Overview**:
  - Incrementally replace parts of a monolithic application with serverless components.
- **Steps**:
  1. Identify a feature or module to migrate (e.g., user authentication).
  2. Implement the module as a serverless component (e.g., Lambda with DynamoDB).
  3. Route traffic to the new component using an API Gateway or reverse proxy.
  4. Gradually replace more components until the monolith is fully replaced.

3. Domain-Driven Design (DDD)

- **Overview**:
  - Break the application into domains or bounded contexts, each representing a business capability.
- **Example**:
  - E-commerce application domains:
    - **Inventory Management**: Serverless workflow using S3, Lambda, and DynamoDB.
    - **Order Processing**: Event-driven architecture with SQS and Lambda.

4. Event-Driven Architecture

- **Overview**:
  - Decouple application components by implementing event-driven communication.
- **Tools**:
  - Amazon SQS, SNS, and EventBridge.
- **Example**:
  - Replace a monolithic checkout process with:
    1. **Order Placed** → SNS notification.

2. **Order Processed** $\rightarrow$ Lambda function updates inventory.

3. **Payment Confirmation** $\rightarrow$ SQS triggers notification service.

5. Database Decoupling

- **Challenge**:
  - Monoliths often rely on a single database for all operations.
- **Solution**:
  - Migrate to purpose-built databases for each microservice:
    - DynamoDB for session storage.
    - RDS for relational data.
    - S3 for file storage.

Real-World Migration Success Stories

1. Netflix

- **Scenario**:

o Netflix faced scalability challenges with their monolithic architecture.

- **Migration**:
  - o Moved to a serverless model using AWS Lambda, DynamoDB, and S3.
- **Outcome**:
  - o Achieved massive scalability, reduced costs, and improved fault tolerance.

---

2. FINRA (Financial Industry Regulatory Authority)

- **Scenario**:
  - o Needed to process billions of stock market events daily.
- **Migration**:
  - o Re-architected systems using AWS Lambda and Kinesis for real-time processing.
- **Outcome**:
  - o Reduced processing costs and improved scalability for high-volume workloads.

---

3. Coca-Cola

- **Scenario**:

- o Required a cost-effective solution for vending machine telemetry.

- **Migration**:
  - o Deployed AWS Lambda to process telemetry data and SNS for notifications.

- **Outcome**:
  - o Reduced operational costs by 60% and enabled real-time data analysis.

---

4. iRobot

- **Scenario**:
  - o IoT devices like Roomba needed real-time command and telemetry processing.

- **Migration**:
  - o Built a serverless architecture using AWS IoT Core, Lambda, and DynamoDB.

- **Outcome**:
  - o Achieved real-time scalability and simplified device management.

Best Practices for Migration

1. **Start Small**:

o Migrate non-critical components or simple workflows first.

2. **Monitor Performance**:

   o Use CloudWatch and X-Ray to monitor and optimize serverless components.

3. **Automate Deployments**:

   o Implement CI/CD pipelines for faster and more reliable deployments.

4. **Ensure Backward Compatibility**:

   o Maintain compatibility with existing systems during phased migrations.

5. **Optimize for Cost**:

   o Use tools like AWS Cost Explorer to monitor and optimize serverless costs.

Migrating legacy applications to serverless can unlock scalability, cost-efficiency, and operational agility. By carefully evaluating feasibility, applying structured migration strategies, and learning from real-world success stories, organizations can achieve a smooth transition to modern, serverless architectures.

Chapter 25: Multi-Cloud and Hybrid Serverless Architectures

Organizations increasingly adopt multi-cloud and hybrid architectures to maximize flexibility, ensure redundancy, and leverage the best features of various platforms. This chapter explores using AWS Lambda in multi-cloud environments, connecting serverless architectures to on-premises systems, and provides real-world examples of hybrid serverless architectures.

Using AWS Lambda in Multi-Cloud Environments

Multi-cloud environments utilize services from multiple cloud providers, allowing organizations to avoid vendor lock-in and optimize for performance and cost.

---

1. Benefits of Multi-Cloud Architectures

- **Resilience and Redundancy**:
  - Spread workloads across providers to reduce dependency on a single vendor.
- **Cost Optimization**:
  - Select cost-effective services for specific use cases from different providers.

- **Access to Best Features**:
  - ○ Leverage unique features from AWS Lambda, Google Cloud Functions, or Azure Functions.

---

2. Challenges of Multi-Cloud Architectures

- **Increased Complexity**:
  - ○ Managing deployments, security, and monitoring across platforms can be challenging.
- **Interoperability**:
  - ○ Ensuring seamless communication between services from different providers requires careful planning.
- **Data Transfer Costs**:
  - ○ Moving data between clouds incurs latency and costs.

---

3. Multi-Cloud Use Cases for AWS Lambda

- **Data Processing**:
  - ○ Process and analyze data in AWS Lambda and share results with Google BigQuery for advanced analytics.
- **Cross-Cloud Event Triggers**:
  - ○ Use AWS EventBridge to trigger Google Cloud Functions or Azure Functions based on AWS events.

---

4. Tools for Multi-Cloud Integration

- **Terraform**:
  - A platform-agnostic Infrastructure-as-Code (IaC) tool for provisioning resources across multiple clouds.
- **Serverless Framework**:
  - Supports deploying serverless functions on multiple providers from a single configuration.
- **Cloud Functions Interoperability**:
  - Use APIs and webhooks to enable communication between serverless functions across clouds.

Connecting Serverless to On-Premises Systems

Hybrid architectures integrate serverless services with on-premises infrastructure, enabling a gradual migration to the cloud or leveraging existing investments.

---

1. Use Cases for Hybrid Architectures

- **Data Processing Pipelines**:
  - Collect and process data from on-premises systems in AWS Lambda.
- **Legacy Application Integration**:

o Extend legacy systems with serverless components for scalability and modernization.

- **IoT Applications**:
  o Process data from on-premises IoT devices using AWS Greengrass and Lambda.

2. Tools for Hybrid Integration

- **AWS Direct Connect**:
  o Provides a high-speed, low-latency connection between on-premises systems and AWS services.
- **AWS Greengrass**:
  o Extends AWS Lambda functionality to edge devices for local data processing.
- **AWS VPN**:
  o Securely connects on-premises networks to AWS.
- **DataSync**:
  o Automates data movement between on-premises storage and AWS services like S3.

3. Workflow Example: Extending On-Premises Systems

- **Scenario**:

- o A legacy ERP system generates sales data stored on-premises.
- **Solution**:
  1. Use AWS DataSync to transfer sales data to S3.
  2. Trigger a Lambda function to process the data and store insights in DynamoDB.
  3. Notify stakeholders using SNS.

Real-World Hybrid Architecture Examples

---

1. Retail Inventory Management

- **Scenario**:
  - o A retail chain uses on-premises systems to manage store inventories.
- **Solution**:
  - o AWS Greengrass processes inventory data locally at each store.
  - o Periodic data sync with Lambda in AWS analyzes inventory trends and restocking needs.
- **Outcome**:
  - o Reduced latency for local operations and centralized insights for decision-making.

2. Financial Services Compliance

- **Scenario**:
  - o A bank stores sensitive customer data on-premises due to compliance regulations but uses AWS for analytics.
- **Solution**:
  - o AWS Direct Connect provides a secure link between the on-premises database and AWS.
  - o Lambda processes data in AWS without storing sensitive information in the cloud.
- **Outcome**:
  - o Compliant and scalable data analytics with minimized data exposure.

3. Multi-Cloud Video Processing

- **Scenario**:
  - o A media company streams videos using both AWS and Google Cloud.
- **Solution**:
  - o Use AWS Lambda to encode video files uploaded to S3.

o Process metadata using Google Cloud Functions and store it in Google BigQuery.

- **Outcome**:
  o Optimized performance and cost-effectiveness by leveraging the strengths of both clouds.

4. IoT Data Aggregation

- **Scenario**:
  o An IoT system generates data from devices located in remote areas with intermittent connectivity.
- **Solution**:
  o AWS Greengrass processes data locally and sends summaries to Lambda for centralized analysis when connectivity is available.
- **Outcome**:
  o Reliable IoT data processing with reduced latency and efficient cloud usage.

Best Practices for Multi-Cloud and Hybrid Architectures

1. **Standardize Infrastructure Management**:
   o Use IaC tools like Terraform for consistent deployment across platforms.

2. **Optimize Data Transfer**:
   - o Minimize inter-cloud or on-premises-to-cloud data transfers to reduce costs and latency.

3. **Monitor Across Environments**:
   - o Implement centralized monitoring using tools like Datadog or CloudWatch with cross-cloud plugins.

4. **Secure Communication**:
   - o Use encrypted channels (e.g., HTTPS, VPN) for all inter-cloud and hybrid communications.

5. **Leverage Cloud-Agnostic Frameworks**:
   - o Use frameworks like Serverless Framework to simplify multi-cloud deployments.

Multi-cloud and hybrid serverless architectures combine the strengths of various platforms to provide flexibility, scalability, and cost optimization. By leveraging AWS Lambda with other cloud providers or on-premises systems, organizations can build resilient and efficient solutions. Following best practices and real-world examples, this chapter equips you to design and implement advanced serverless architectures.

Chapter 26: Advanced Use Cases for AWS Lambda

AWS Lambda's versatility extends beyond traditional use cases to power advanced applications such as media processing pipelines, chatbots, and more. This chapter explores how to implement image and video processing pipelines, build chatbots using Lambda and Amazon Lex, and provides real-world examples of advanced Lambda solutions.

Image and Video Processing Pipelines

Serverless architectures are ideal for processing images and videos due to their ability to handle high concurrency and event-driven workflows.

---

1. Image Processing with AWS Lambda

- **Scenario**:
    - A photo-sharing platform requires automated image resizing and format conversion.
- **Workflow**:
1. Users upload images to an S3 bucket.
    2. S3 triggers a Lambda function to process the image.

3. Processed images are stored in a separate S3 bucket for retrieval.

- **Code Example** (Image Resizing):

python

```python
import boto3
from PIL import Image
import io

s3 = boto3.client('s3')

def lambda_handler(event, context):
    bucket = event['Records'][0]['s3']['bucket']['name']
    key = event['Records'][0]['s3']['object']['key']

    # Download the image
    response = s3.get_object(Bucket=bucket, Key=key)
    image = Image.open(io.BytesIO(response['Body'].read()))

    # Resize the image
    resized_image = image.resize((200, 200))

    # Save the resized image to a buffer
    buffer = io.BytesIO()
    resized_image.save(buffer, format='JPEG')
    buffer.seek(0)

    # Upload the processed image
```

```
s3.put_object(Bucket='processed-images-bucket',      Key=f'resized-{key}', Body=buffer)
    return {'statusCode': 200, 'body': 'Image processed successfully'}
```

- **Best Practices**:

  - Use Lambda layers for shared libraries like PIL or OpenCV.

  - Optimize function memory allocation for large image processing tasks.

2. Video Processing with AWS Lambda

- **Scenario**:

  - A streaming platform processes videos into multiple resolutions for adaptive streaming.

- **Workflow**:

1. Videos are uploaded to an S3 bucket.

    2. S3 triggers a Lambda function that invokes AWS Elastic Transcoder or AWS MediaConvert to process the videos.

    3. Transcoded videos are stored in an S3 bucket for delivery.

- **Code Example** (Using Elastic Transcoder):

python

```python
import boto3

transcoder = boto3.client('elastictranscoder')

def lambda_handler(event, context):
    pipeline_id = 'your-pipeline-id'
    bucket = event['Records'][0]['s3']['bucket']['name']
    key = event['Records'][0]['s3']['object']['key']

    response = transcoder.create_job(
        PipelineId=pipeline_id,
        Input={'Key': key},
        Outputs=[
            {'Key': f'{key}-1080p.mp4', 'PresetId': '1351620000001-
000001'}, # 1080p
            {'Key': f'{key}-720p.mp4', 'PresetId': '1351620000001-
000010'}, # 720p
        ]
    )
    return {'statusCode': 200, 'body': 'Video processing started'}
```

- **Best Practices**:
  - o Use asynchronous workflows with SQS or EventBridge for high-volume video processing.
  - o Optimize cost by transcoding only requested resolutions.

Building Chatbots with Lambda and Amazon Lex

Amazon Lex provides natural language understanding (NLU) and automatic speech recognition (ASR) for building conversational interfaces. AWS Lambda complements Lex by handling business logic.

1. Overview of Lex and Lambda Integration

- **Amazon Lex**:
    - Handles intent recognition and natural language processing.
- **AWS Lambda**:
    - Executes backend logic for fulfilling user intents.

2. Steps to Build a Chatbot

- **Step 1: Design the Lex Bot**
    1. Define intents (e.g., BookAppointment, GetWeather).
    2. Add slots (parameters) to collect from the user (e.g., date, time).
    3. Configure responses for different scenarios.
- **Step 2: Connect Lambda for Fulfillment**
    - Lambda executes logic for the intents.
    - Example (Booking Appointments):

    python

```python
def lambda_handler(event, context):
    intent_name = event['currentIntent']['name']

    if intent_name == 'BookAppointment':
        slots = event['currentIntent']['slots']
        date = slots['Date']
        time = slots['Time']
        return {
            'dialogAction': {
                'type': 'Close',
                'fulfillmentState': 'Fulfilled',
                'message': {'contentType': 'PlainText', 'content':
f'Appointment booked for {date} at {time}'}
            }
        }
```

- **Step 3: Test the Bot**
  - o Use the Lex console or integrate with platforms like Slack, Facebook Messenger, or a custom web UI.

---

3. Real-World Chatbot Use Cases

- **Customer Support**:
  - o Automate FAQs and troubleshooting.
- **E-Commerce**:
  - o Assist customers in finding products or tracking orders.

- **Healthcare**:
  - Schedule appointments or provide medication reminders.

Real-World Examples of Advanced Lambda Solutions

---

1. Real-Time Fraud Detection

- **Scenario**:
  - A payment gateway detects fraudulent transactions.
- **Solution**:
  1. Transactions are processed by Lambda.
  2. Anomaly detection models hosted on SageMaker identify fraud.
  3. SNS alerts the security team for flagged transactions.
- **Outcome**:
  - Reduced fraud incidents and real-time decision-making.

---

2. IoT Data Processing

- **Scenario**:

- o IoT sensors send temperature and humidity data to the cloud.
- **Solution**:
  1. IoT Core routes messages to Lambda.
  2. Lambda processes data and stores it in DynamoDB.
  3. High thresholds trigger SNS notifications.
- **Outcome**:
  - o Real-time monitoring of environmental conditions.

---

3. Personalized Recommendations

- **Scenario**:
  - o An e-commerce platform offers product recommendations.
- **Solution**:
  1. User activity is logged in DynamoDB.
  2. Lambda triggers personalized recommendations using a SageMaker model.
  3. Recommendations are displayed to the user.
- **Outcome**:
  - o Increased customer engagement and sales.

Best Practices for Advanced Lambda Solutions

1. **Use Event-Driven Architecture**:
   - o Leverage S3, DynamoDB Streams, and EventBridge for efficient workflows.

2. **Optimize for Performance**:
   - o Allocate appropriate memory and monitor execution times.

3. **Secure Sensitive Data**:
   - o Use IAM roles, encryption, and Secrets Manager for secure operations.

4. **Monitor and Debug**:
   - o Use CloudWatch Logs and AWS X-Ray to monitor and debug complex workflows.

5. **Scale Efficiently**:
   - o Design applications to handle high concurrency with minimal latency.

AWS Lambda powers advanced use cases such as media processing, chatbot development, and real-time analytics. By integrating Lambda with services like Amazon Lex and SageMaker, organizations can build innovative and scalable solutions. Following the workflows and best practices outlined in this chapter, you can unlock the full potential of AWS Lambda for complex, high-impact applications.

Chapter 27: The Future of Serverless and AWS Lambda

Serverless computing has revolutionized how applications are built and deployed, and its evolution continues to shape the future of cloud computing. This chapter explores trends in serverless computing, innovations on AWS and beyond, and how developers and organizations can prepare for the ever-changing serverless landscape.

Trends in Serverless Computing
Serverless computing is maturing, with emerging trends aimed at addressing challenges and expanding use cases.

---

1. Expanding Beyond Functions

- **Beyond AWS Lambda**:
    - Modern serverless platforms are incorporating broader services such as managed databases, storage, and AI.
    - Example: AWS Aurora Serverless for on-demand database scalability.
- **Serverless Containers**:

- o Platforms like AWS Fargate offer serverless container orchestration, blending serverless simplicity with container flexibility.

2. Edge Computing Integration

- **Trend**:
  - o Running serverless workloads closer to end users for reduced latency.
- **Examples**:
  - o AWS Lambda@Edge processes requests at CloudFront locations.
  - o Cloudflare Workers enable serverless functions at the edge.

3. Event-Driven Architectures

- **Trend**:
  - o Serverless computing aligns naturally with event-driven patterns, enabling real-time data processing.
- **Examples**:
  - o AWS EventBridge simplifies building event buses for decoupled architectures.

4. AI and Machine Learning Integration

- **Trend**:
  - o Serverless computing increasingly supports AI/ML workloads.
- **Examples**:
  - o Running inference tasks with serverless platforms like Lambda or SageMaker.
  - o Automating training pipelines with serverless workflows.

---

5. Green Computing and Sustainability

- **Trend**:
  - o Focus on energy-efficient computing with serverless, as resources are used only when needed.
- **Examples**:
  - o AWS's focus on renewable energy and carbon-efficient infrastructure.

Innovations on AWS and Beyond

The serverless ecosystem is evolving rapidly, with AWS leading the way and competitors innovating in parallel.

1. AWS Lambda Innovations

- **Improved Cold Start Performance**:
  - o AWS has reduced cold start latency, especially for provisioned concurrency.
- **Graviton2 Support**:
  - o Lambda supports AWS Graviton2 processors, offering better performance and cost savings.
- **Lambda SnapStart**:
  - o Accelerates cold start times by snapshotting function states for faster initialization.
- **Expanded Runtime Support**:
  - o Lambda now supports languages like Rust, Java, Python, Node.js, and custom runtimes.

2. Competitor Innovations

- **Google Cloud Functions**:
  - o Enhanced integration with Google Cloud's AI/ML tools.
- **Microsoft Azure Functions**:
  - o Built-in support for Azure Durable Functions, enabling stateful serverless workflows.
- **Cloudflare Workers**:

 o Focus on edge computing with ultra-low latency.

---

3. Third-Party Tools and Frameworks

- **Serverless Framework**:
  - o Simplifies multi-cloud serverless deployments.
- **Terraform**:
  - o Infrastructure-as-code tool for consistent deployments across providers.
- **Pulumi**:
  - o Enables developers to use familiar programming languages for infrastructure management.

Preparing for the Evolving Serverless Landscape

As serverless computing continues to grow, developers and organizations must adapt to leverage its full potential.

---

1. Adopt a Multi-Cloud Mindset

- **Why It Matters**:
  - o Avoid vendor lock-in and leverage the best features of multiple providers.
- **How to Prepare**:

- o Learn cloud-agnostic tools like Terraform and Serverless Framework.

2. Focus on Event-Driven Design

- **Why It Matters**:
  - o Event-driven architectures enable scalability and flexibility.
- **How to Prepare**:
  - o Design systems around event sources like S3, EventBridge, and DynamoDB Streams.

3. Upskill in Edge Computing

- **Why It Matters**:
  - o Edge computing supports use cases requiring ultra-low latency.
- **How to Prepare**:
  - o Explore AWS Lambda@Edge, Cloudflare Workers, and Akamai EdgeWorkers.

4. Learn AI and ML Integration

- **Why It Matters**:

- o AI/ML workloads are increasingly integrated with serverless.
- **How to Prepare**:
  - o Gain proficiency in services like SageMaker, Google AutoML, and TensorFlow.js.

5. Prioritize Security and Compliance

- **Why It Matters**:
  - o Serverless introduces unique security challenges, such as managing ephemeral resources.
- **How to Prepare**:
  - o Implement IAM best practices, use AWS Secrets Manager, and adopt tools like AWS Config for compliance monitoring.

6. Embrace Observability and Monitoring

- **Why It Matters**:
  - o Observability is critical for managing distributed serverless applications.
- **How to Prepare**:
  - o Use tools like AWS X-Ray, CloudWatch Logs Insights, and Datadog for end-to-end monitoring.

7. Experiment with Emerging Use Cases

- **Why It Matters**:
  - Serverless computing is being applied to new domains, such as blockchain and quantum computing.
- **How to Prepare**:
  - Stay informed about experimental features like Amazon Braket for quantum computing.

The Road Ahead: Realizing the Full Potential of Serverless

The future of serverless computing promises greater integration across clouds, lower operational overhead, and broader adoption of advanced technologies like AI and edge computing. Developers and organizations that embrace these innovations will be well-positioned to drive impactful solutions in the years ahead.